PACIFIC ELECTRIC

In Color

VOLUME I
P. Allen Copeland

THE PACIFIC ELECTRIC RAILWAY

In Color

THE LAST YEARS OF THE "BIG RED CARS"

Published by
MORNING SUN BOOKS, INC.
9 Pheasant Lane
Scotch Plains, NJ 07076

Library of Congress
Catalog Card No. 97-073625

First Printing
ISBN 1-878887-88-2

Color separation and printing by
The Kutztown Publishing Co., Inc.
Kutztown, Pennsylvania

DEDICATION

Dedicated to my best friend and wife of 31-years, Virginia.

I have been fascinated with the Pacific Electric since first sighting the Newport Line in 1945 while on a trip from San Diego to visit a cousin in Long Beach. The "Big Red Cars" were so much more impressive than the San Diego streetcars I was used to, and the electric locomotives, box motors and enormous array of services led to a lasting fascination with this company. Since that time I have endeavored to study, understand and savor this large commercial enterprise, which was not only a major commercial operation but also a motivating force in the development of Los Angeles, Orange and the Eastern portions of San Bernardino and Riverside Counties in Southern California.

Much has been written and published on the Pacific Electric Railway. Indeed, a bibliography of the railway is quite possibly the largest of any electric railroad. A majority of this material was published due to the efforts of the late Ira Swett, who wrote and published prodigious amounts of historical and interesting material on the P.E. His enthusiasm for the history of Los Angeles and the railway was contagious, and affected many others who have contributed to our knowledge of the railway. Even with all this material, many subjects and aspects of the railway remain to be explored. Since the death of Mr. Swett in 1975, publications on the P.E. have fallen off, and the last was published in 1991. Aside from short articles published by the Orange Empire Railway Museum and the Electric Railway Historical Society of Southern California, little has been written in recent years on the P.E. at a time when it is important to understand transportation in the recent past while new links are proposed, restudied, financed and constructed. Following in the footsteps of Ira Swett, Donald Duke, Charles Seims, Eli Bail, Jeff Moreau, Mac Sebree, Jim Walker, Ray Long, Ray Younghans and others in documenting the P.E. is a daunting task, but I hope that this effort will be as interesting and inspirational to others as those people have been to me.

This is not a history or thorough review of the Pacific Electric. This is a color pictorial of the P.E. empire in the late years of its existence. While much of the rail system remained intact in the years following World War Two, color film was not extensively used by railfan photographers until later availability and price declines made the medium a popular one to preserve the images of familiar subjects. In the last years of P.E. operations, a few pioneering and far sighted individuals sought to record images of the system before the familiar and commonplace disappeared.

I have attempted to select as many representative views as possible. However, not all locations or subjects seem to have been photographed and/or made available to the writer.

Especially needed are shots of the Class 1500 suburban locomotives, non-powered freight and maintenance of way equipment and motor coaches. Hopefully, additional photographic material will be forthcoming to augment the slides that are being assembled for future volumes on the "World's Greatest Interurban System".

Special mention must be made of the encouragement, broad scope of knowledge, engineering discipline and considerable material assistance that has been provided to the writer by Ken Douglas. Jim Buckley, through his friendship provided me with the model and inspiration to write about traction subjects. Joe Strapac, one of the most prolific and knowledgeable writers/publishers on the Southern Pacific and its motive power, was a catalyst in prodding me to "do something on the lines P.E." Thanks fellows. I would also like to mention those who have been of particular inspirational or material assistance on this project:

Eli Bail, Ray Ballash, Kurt Brokhausen, Jim Buckley, Herb Cearly, Ken Douglas, Donald Duke, Pat Ellyson, Dave Garcia, Jim Gibson, Sanford Goodrick, Emery Gulash, Jim Harrison, William C. Janssen, John Kirchner, Fred Matthews, Edward S. Miller, Wally Shidler, Dick Stephenson, Henry Stange, Joe Strapac, Jim Walker, Ray Younghans, and, of course, Morning Sun Books publisher Bob Yanosey.

There are also many others who have helped me in innumerable ways, but unfortunately it is impossible to list them all, and to them I apologize. To all of you I offer my must sincere appreciation and gratitude. I would also like to acknowledge the preservation efforts of the founders and members of the Orange Empire Railway Museum, at Perris, Calif. Through their time, treasure and physical efforts they have managed to preserve for the future not only rolling stock of the Pacific Electric, but also the physical aspects and feeling of a real electric railway.

P. Allen Copeland
May 28, 1997

3

The Pacific Electric was once the largest and most varied electric railroad in North America, and developed growth patters in Southern California that are still being felt today. Principally a freight carrier (the third biggest carrier in California), the company also was the operator of interurban, suburban and local passenger service. The rail vehicles were known as the "Big Red Cars" by employees and patrons alike.

During the early years of the Pacific Electric, public transportation was vital to the growth and development of the metropolitan area. Indeed many of the predecessor companies of the Pacific Electric were built to stimulate real estate ventures. In 1911 when the Southern Pacific bought these companies and combined them into the "new" Pacific Electric Ry. the emphasis gradually changed. SP desired that the company place importance on the development of freight traffic that would feed traffic onto the railroad. During the 1920s and 1930s, the automobile became the dominant vehicle of transportation in Southern California, a factor which has continued to the present day. With the rise of ownership of automobiles, P.E. passenger service assumed a subordinate role. The company attempted to adapt to changing conditions with new equipment and use of the motor bus, first to open up new areas of traffic, to replace minor (money losing) streetcar lines in outlying communities, as a feeder service to the rail lines and as a replacement for them later. The company's desire to be rid of many passenger only rail and bus lines can be shown easily by the sale of the complete Pasadena and Glendale operations in 1941. Other local routes in Long Beach and San Bernardino were abandoned and not replaced by bus service at all.

World War Two temporarily halted the decline of passenger service on the P.E. and once again public transportation assumed an indispensable part of the economic and social fabric of the Los Angeles metropolitan area. This situation was not entirely beneficial, as labor shortages developed due to employees being needed for the war effort, equipment and track was heavily used and upkeep of facilities could not be maintained. However, the Pacific Electric was able to handle a wartime traffic increase of 280% in one year, which indicates that considerable excess capacity existed. These high traffic levels could not last, and when war time shortages disappeared, people returned to their automobiles. Passenger service declined, and increasing costs forced a series of service reductions and fare increases. These measures in turn caused further declines. However, it wasn't until 1949 that a renewed program began in earnest to reduce costs and to replace a majority of the rail lines with diesel buses. Many plans for "rapid transit" were advanced during this time, but the P.E. stated that it did not have the resources to upgrade the rail passenger network or to operate such a system. Even as quickly as the P.E. desired to replace rail lines with buses, they were forced to abandon even more quickly several profitable rail lines so that freeways could be constructed. The City of Los Angeles was ambivalent about the conversion program, and there was no leadership at the public level to to support modernization with coordination or funding that is typical today. It was obvious that the Pacific Electric could operate buses on public streets and roads paid for by the taxpayers. Property taxes were levied on the private rights of way and facilities used by the Red Cars, the rights of way were also being cut through for new roads, slowing the rail cars down. The passenger rail system was doomed by these pressures, which at times seemed to be coordinated. With a renewed desire by the Southern Pacific to concentrate on freight, the ultimate answer was to sell all the passenger service to Metropolitan Coach Lines, owned by a San Diego holding company that operated a number of urban transit systems in the West. Metro Coach immediately announced plans for the replacement of all rail passenger service and did convert lines to Hollywood and Glendale-Burbank. However, opposing pressures kept four lines operating until 1958, when a public agency, the Los Angeles Metropolitan Transit Authority acquired the assets of transit operators in the Los Angeles area. What P.E. and Metro Coach couldn't do, the M.T.A. accomplished quickly, and in 1961 the last interurban rail line to Long Beach was abandoned.

It is ironic that the descendant of this public agency spent millions of dollars to restore electric rail passenger service over the same route of the Long Beach line in 1990, which is operating as the Metro Blue Line. The P.E. continued to provide freight service on the rail lines that were retained until August 13, 1965 when the railway was absorbed into the Southern Pacific. The SP was purchased in 1996 by the Union Pacific Railroad.

As of January 1, 1945, the Pacific Electric operated 904-miles of track, and owned 483 passenger cars. For passenger service these were supplemented with 334 motor coaches. For freight, the following equipment was operated:

Electric locomotives	44
Steam locomotives	19
Diesel electric locomotives	6
Gas electric locomotives	2
Box motors	41
RPO-Express cars	3
Non-powered freight cars	1662

49 electrical substations were owned, and 300-miles of transmission lines used to connect them to the electrical overhead that powered much of the freight and passenger service.

PACIFIC ELECTRIC RAIL LINES

In January 1943, the Pacific Electric assigned route numbers to their passenger services.
Note that the assigned line numbers never appeared on any of the rail cars
operated by P.E. or its successor, Metropolitan Coach Lines.
Under P.E.'s numbering system, lines were grouped as rail or bus, local or interurban:

INTERURBAN RAIL LINES:

1 Los Angeles-Pasadena via Oak Knoll. Replaced by bus service Oct. 8, 1950.

2 Los Angeles-Pasadena via Short Line. Replaced by bus service Sept. 30, 1951.

3 Los Angeles-El Monte-Baldwin Park-Covina. Cut back to Baldwin Park on March 28, 1947. Replaced by bus service Oct. 15, 1950.

4 Los Angeles-Monrovia-Glendora. Replaced by bus service Sept. 30, 1951.

5 Los Angeles-Sierra Madre. Replaced by bus service Oct. 6, 1950.

6 Los Angeles-Long Beach. Sold to Metropolitan Coach Lines Oct. 1. 1953. Sold to Los Angeles Metropolitan Transit Authority March 3, 1958. Replaced by bus service April 9, 1961. A new Los Angeles-Long Beach electric rail line started July 16, 1990, and the bus service that had replaced the red cars was abandoned on June 23, 1991.

7 Los Angeles-San Pedro. Sold to Metropolitan Coach Lines Oct. 1, 1953. Sold to Los Angeles Metropolitan Transit Authority March 3, 1958. Replaced by bus service Dec. 7, 1958.

8 Los Angeles-Catalina Dock special steamship service. Sold to Metropolitan Coach Lines Oct. 1, 1953. Sold to Los Angeles Metropolitan Transit Authority May 3, 1958. Abandoned October 12, 1958.

9 Long Beach-San Pedro. Replaced by bus Jan. 2, 1949.

10 Long Beach-Catalina Dock special steamship service. Abandoned April 30, 1949.

11 Los Angeles-Santa Ana. Cut back to Bellflower on July 2, 1950. Sold to Metropolitan Coach Lines Oct. 1, 1953; sold to Metropolitan Coach Lines May 3, 1958. Replaced by bus May 25, 1958. Red car replacement bus discontinued June 23, 1991. Patrons to use new Los Angeles-Long Beach electric line with connecting buses. Establishment of new electric light rail line in the middle of the Century Freeway (called the "Green Line") used a portion of the old Bellflower line right of way. This service started August 14, 1995.

12 Los Angeles-Santa Monica via Air Line. One run a day franchise service abandoned October 26, 1953.

13 Los Angeles-Newport Beach special service. Abandoned May 2, 1943 and replaced by line 17.

14 Los Angeles-San Bernardino special service. Discontinued Aug. 1944.

15 Los Angeles-Terminal Island. Established March 19, 1943. Abandoned Sept. 16, 1945.

16 Long Beach-Terminal Island. Established March 19, 1943. Abandoned Sept. 16, 1945.

17 Los Angeles-Newport Beach. Established May 2, 1943. Partial summer service operated 1945, and rush hour service from June 17, 1946. Saturday service abandoned April 8, 1950, weekday service abandoned June 30, 1950.

LOS ANGELES LOCAL RAIL LINES:

25 Watts-Sierra Vista. Split Oct. 22, 1950 into lines 25 and 26.

25" Los Angeles-Watts. Established Oct. 22, 1950. Sold to Metropolitan Coach Lines Oct. 1, 1953. Sold to Los Angeles Metropolitan Transit Authority March 3, 1958. Replaced by bus Oct. 2, 1959.

26 Hollywood-Blvd.-Venice Short Line. Split April 18, 1943 into lines 30 and 31.

26" Los Angeles-Sierra Vista. Established Oct. 22, 1950. Replaced by bus Sept. 30, 1951.

27 Subway Terminal-Hollywood Blvd. Combined June 1, 1943 into line 32.

28 Subway Terminal-Santa Monica Blvd.-West Hollywood/San Fernando Valley. Split Oct. 1, 1950 into lines 28 and 33.

28" Subway Terminal-Santa Monica Blvd.-West Hollywood. Established Oct. 1, 1950. Replaced by bus June 1, 1953.

29 Subway Terminal-Glendale-Burbank. Sold to Metropolitan Coach Lines Oct. 1, 1953. Replaced by bus June 19, 1955.

30 Venice Short Line (Los-Angeles-Venice-Santa Monica). Established April 18, 1943. Replaced by bus Sept. 17, 1950.

31 Hollywood Blvd.-San Vicente Blvd. Established April 18, 1943. Combined June 1, 1943 with line 32.

32 Subway Terminal-Hollywood Blvd.-West Hollywood; 11th & Hill-Hollywood Blvd.-Gardner St.* Routes 32 and 31 merged on June 1, 1943. Local service on surface tracks from 11th and Hill abandoned Oct. 1, 1950. Subway Terminal-Hollywood Blvd.-West Hollywood service sold to Metropolitan Coach Lines Oct. 1, 1953. Replaced by bus Sept. 26, 1954.

33 Subway Terminal-Santa Monica Blvd.-San Fernando Valley. Established October 1, 1950. Replaced by bus Dec. 28, 1952.

* *(Included Echo Penn Ave. Local Line)*

5

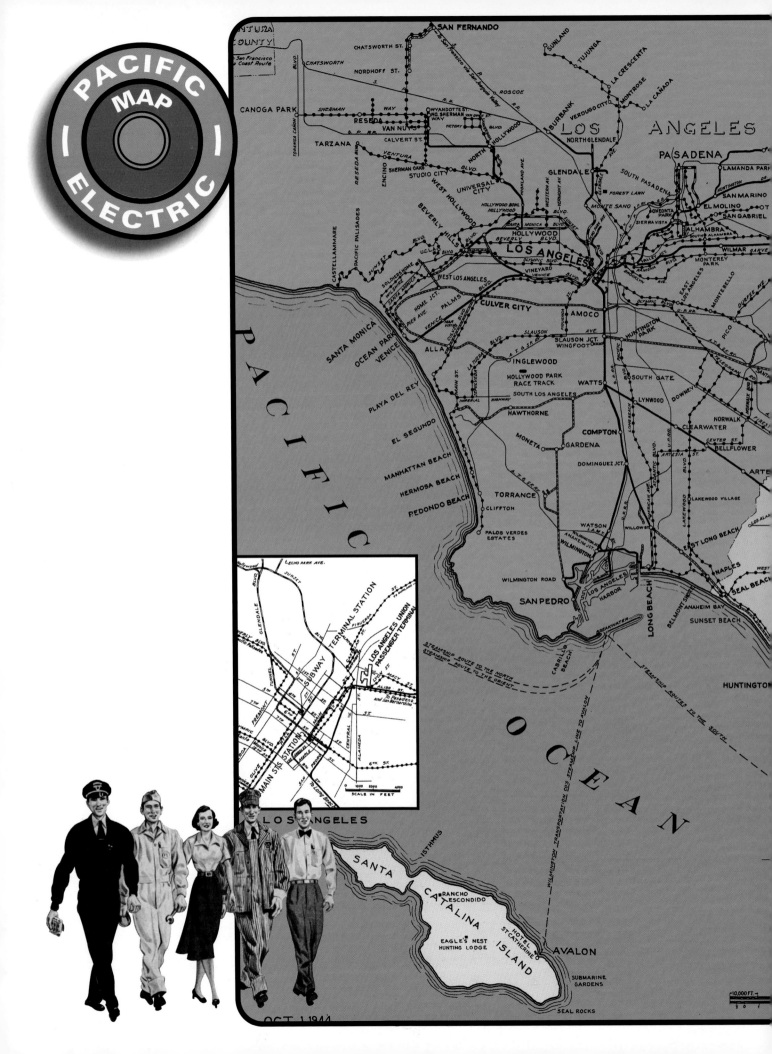

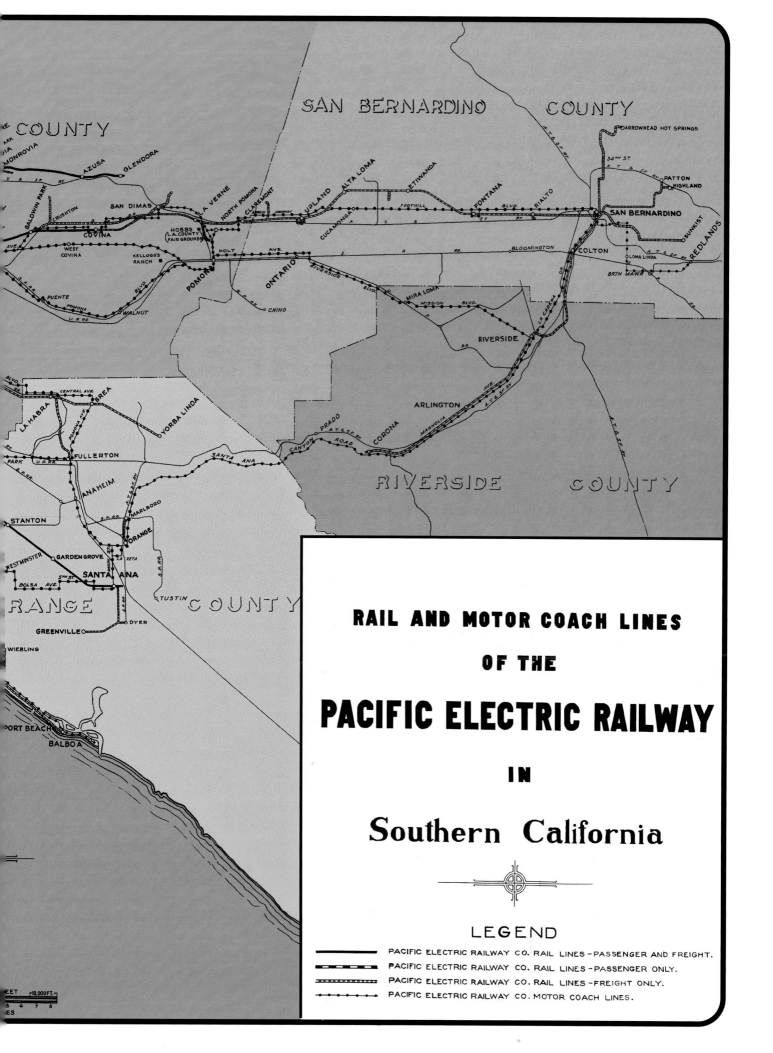

RAIL AND MOTOR COACH LINES

OF THE

PACIFIC ELECTRIC RAILWAY

IN

Southern California

LEGEND

—————————— PACIFIC ELECTRIC RAILWAY CO. RAIL LINES – PASSENGER AND FREIGHT.

— — — — — PACIFIC ELECTRIC RAILWAY CO. RAIL LINES – PASSENGER ONLY.

··················· PACIFIC ELECTRIC RAILWAY CO. RAIL LINES – FREIGHT ONLY.

•—•—•—•—• PACIFIC ELECTRIC RAILWAY CO. MOTOR COACH LINES.

Pacific Electric's smallest all steel double truck cars was the 100-series. Comprised of 15 cars built by St. Louis in 1930, the group was intended for streetcar service in Long Beach, San Bernardino and Riverside. The cars also saw operation in Pasadena and on shuttle operations in Los Angeles. When those lines were abandoned or sold in 1940-41, most of the class was modernized and assigned to the Echo Park Ave. Local Line on August 15, 1942. They were joined in 1943 by the cars from the abandoned Riverside-Arlington line. No. 103 is shown inbound on the Echo Park Ave. line very near the northern end on September 4, 1950. *(Ken Douglas)*

The Echo Park Ave. line operated over Echo Park Ave., Sunset Blvd. and Hill Street. On Hill Street, the line operated on right of way through two tunnels. No. 109 is leaving the north Hill Street Tunnel on an inbound Echo Park Ave. run. The southbound car will soon cross Temple Street on Jan. 11, 1950. *(Ken Douglas)*

Nos. 100-114 were assigned to the Western District of the PE after 1943, and were primarily used on the Echo Park Ave. Local line. This line operated from a crossover at 11th and Hill Sts, and operated north through two tunnels to Sunset Blvd. and thence to Echo Park Ave. On Echo Park Ave., most of the line was single track with passing sidings. Nos. 113 and 102 are shown passing at the Marsden Ave. siding on Echo Park Ave. on Jan. 11, 1950. *(Ken Douglas)*

From April 18, 1943, one car was assigned to the Vineyard-San Vicente Shuttle, working nights and Sundays. The small car and one-man operation caused significant cost savings over the two man cars then operated on the Venice Blvd. Local Line. 100's were also used on other Western District lines on special occasions, such as New Year's Day (when they ran into the subway on the Santa Monica Blvd.-Subway line) and on fan trips. No. 110 is shown on September 4, 1950 while assigned to the shuttle operation at Vineyard, where connection was made with the Venice Short Line and Venice Blvd. local streetcars. *(Ken Douglas)*

On October 1, 1950 the Vineyard-San Vicente shuttle and the Echo Park Ave. local line were replaced by buses. Having no other suitable assignments for the little cars, all were sold in 1950 to Vera Cruz, Mexico. All were converted to single end, and examples were still running in 1981 when that system finally shut down. No. 114 is shown here at the terminal crossover at 11th and Hill Sts. on August 2, 1950 shortly before service on the Echo Park Ave. line ended. *(Jim Buckley)*

PE's largest class of equipment was the 600-class, comprised of city-suburban cars numbered 600-759. Built in four orders by St. Louis and Brill from 1922 to 1928, the group became known as the "Hollywood Cars" because of their assignment to service to that area of Los Angeles. However, they were also assigned to all major city lines, all suburban lines and even interurban lines (after their 1939-40 modernization). This rebuilding was a result of public and political pressure to modernize the equipment used on the PE's rail lines. Car No. 604, from nos. 600-649 built by St. Louis in 1922 is shown here on August 1, 1950 running southbound on the Watts Local Line at Wingfoot Junction on the Southern District *(Jim Buckley)*

No. 617, also from the first group of Hollywood cars (600-649) is shown here running inbound from Sierra Vista just north of Valley Junction in April, 1948. The car will run through downtown Los Angeles passing the Main Street Station and will then run over the Southern District four tracks to terminate at Watts. Because of heavy freight traffic on the Southern District, the Watts-Sierra Vista line will be split in two on October 26, 1950. Operating from the elevated tracks at Main Street Station, the Sierra Vista line will be converted to one-man operation, while the Watts line will continue to operate with a motorman and conductor *(Ken Douglas)*

The second group of Hollywood cars were nos. 650-699, built by St. Louis in 1923. The cars exhibited subtle differences from the earlier group, but were basically similar and could operated in multiple unit with the 1922 cars. Exhibiting this capability, No. 677 and train are shown outbound on the Venice Short Line at Vineyard in December, 1948. Vineyard contained a small yard to store cars for the Venice Blvd.-Hollywood Blvd. Local Line and the Venice Short Line. Limited storage capacity at the Hill Street Station required that some cars be deadheaded to the Station prior to entering service. Just West of the Sears store in the background, was the western terminal loop of the Los Angeles Transit Lines "P" line served by PCC cars. This line, which connected with the buses of the Santa Monica Municipal Bus Line was a fierce competitor for the P.E. *(Emery Gulash)*.

PE 686 is shown on September 12, 1949 with train outbound on the Venice Short Line on Venice Blvd. Ahead is Vineyard and the start of an extensive stretch of private right of way which extends to the outskirts of the terminal in Santa Monica.
(Henry Stange)

The third group of Hollywood cars were nos. 700-749, built by Brill in 1924. These cars were similar to nos. 650-699. In 1938, nos. 735-749 were speeded up for service between the Subway Terminal and Van Nuys. Given faster motors, new destination signs and a distinctive paint job, the cars became known as "Valley Sevens". The cars ran in their own little class until 1939-40 when they were further upgraded with the rest of the Hollywood cars. No. 740 is shown at Venice Blvd. and Rosedale running on the Venice Blvd.-Hollywood Blvd. Local Line on August 1, 1950. The Venice Blvd.-Hill St.-Sunset Blvd. portion of this route would be replaced by bus service on October 1, 1950. Service to Hollywood would continue, but all runs would be made to and from the Subway Terminal. *(Jim Buckley)*

No. 703 was another member of the Brill built 700-749 group. The motorman and conductor are enjoying a few minutes of spot time, before starting a run downtown on the Venice Blvd.-Hollywood Blvd. local line on September 13, 1949. Note that the car has just been repainted even though the 5050 conversion and rehabilitation program of the Hollywood cars is in process. *(Henry Stange)*

The fourth group of Hollywood cars were nos. 750-759, built by St. Louis in 1928. As built, this group contained many differences from the earlier Hollywood cars and were kept separate from them until the modernization of 1939-40. After that, they were considered an integral part of the entire class. No. 750 is shown leaving Main Street Station On June 6, 1951 outbound on the Watts Local Line. A stored "Blimp" and the P.E. motor coach loading deck can be seen at the left. *(Sanford Goodrick)*

While much of the route was forced to run on slow street track, the outer sections of the Subway-Van Nuys line were on private right of way. The track north of Hollywood over Cahuenga Pass was on a right of way installed in the middle of the Hollywood Freeway before World War Two. No. 704 and train are shown inbound at Barham Blvd. on September 13, 1949 in a view by Henry Stange. Rail service would continue to run here until December 28, 1952. The right of way was soon replaced with two additional freeway lanes. *(Henry Stange)*

While the 950's and 1000-series saw much use on the Venice Short Line after World War Two, base service was provided by Hollywood cars. No. 706 is shown outbound on the VSL at Culver Junction. The switch in the foreground is a connection to the Santa Monica Air Line, over which no. 706 will soon cross on May 1, 1949. *(Ken Douglas)*

PE No. 721 leading a two-car outbound train on the Venice Short Line on Hill Street just north of 5th Street. The train has just entered onto Hill Street from the Subway Terminal surface tracks. The overhead leading into the surface tracks can be seen in the background. *(Ken Douglas)*

During World War Two and well into the late 1940's, most of the 600-class were used on the Western District, being used on every line of that service area. However, they did not see exclusive use, as some service was provided by the 100's, the PCC cars, and the 950 and 1000-class interurban cars. Operating on the Hollywood Blvd.-Sunset Blvd.-Hill Street local line, car 738 is southbound on Hill Street, approaching the crossover at 11th where the run will terminate. The car will change ends at the crossover for a return trip to Hollywood. *(Ken Douglas)*

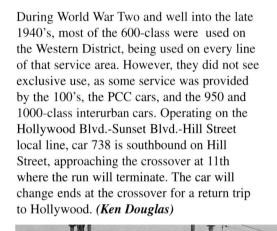

No. 732 and train are shown outbound on Venice Blvd. on March 20, 1949 with a Venice Short Line train. *(Emery Gulash)*

On the P.E. Hollywood-Vineyard line (and the Echo Park line) P.E. tracks ran through two short tunnels that paralleled Hill Street. PE No. 745 is entering into the south Hill Street Tunnel on a Hollywood-Vineyard run in a view taken just inside the tunnel on September 4, 1950. *(Ken Douglas)*

PE No. 746 is seen running on the Venice Blvd.-Hollywood Blvd. local line on August 1, 1950 inbound on Venice Blvd. and Catalina. The line has two more months to operate before being converted to motor coach on October 1, 1950. After the abandonment, the car will be used on the Watts local line and in interurban service to Monrovia-Glendora. *(Jim Buckley)*

After the abandonment of the Venice Short Line and Echo Park Ave. local line, PE ran a weekday franchise car over these lines (from October 1, 1950). No. 752 as the last Venice Short Line franchise car is about to leave on the last outbound run at Marshall Manor. At this point, the line had been severed by a sewer excavation, and passengers had to walk between car 5112 in the background to the 752. *(Ken Douglas)*

PE 752 is about to leave the Broadway station in Santa Monica as the last Venice Short Line franchise car on December 28, 1950. The dog in the front door belonged to the railfan motorman. *(Ken Douglas)*

On the outer section of the Venice Short Line in the Venice area, the PE ran on a private right of way called the "Trolleyway". No. 754 and train are shown inbound on the Trolleyway on November 11, 1949. *(Ken Douglas)*

PE No. 756 is shown at the end of the Monrovia-Glendora line in Glendora. The car was one of the last unconverted 600 type cars in operation. Nos. 600- 731 were converted to the 5050 class in 1949-51, but nos. 732-759 were not rebuilt and remained two-man cars for Watts and Monrovia-Glendora Line service. This group of cars replaced the 1100-series cars on the Glendora line on March 19, 1951 and provided all service on that line until it was converted to motor coach on September 30, 1951. Photographed on September 19, 1951, the car only has a few more days to run in P.E. service. Nos. 732-759 were placed in storage after the abandonment of the Monrovia-Glendora line and were sold later that year to the General Urquiza Ry. in Argentina. A few cars of this group are believed to still exist there as work cars. *(Ken Douglas)*

In 1949-51, PE again rebuilt and modernized cars 600-731 to make them suitable for operation as one-man or two-man cars. As the cars were rebuilt, they were renumbered 5050-5181 (not in order). The cars were compatible with the unrebuilt cars, and could train with them in service. The Glendale-Burbank line was converted to one-man operation on Jan. 7, 1950. The LA-Santa Monica Blvd.-West Hollywood and LA-Santa Monica Blvd.-Van Nuys (San Fernando Valley) lines followed on August 13, 1950. The Sierra Vista Local Line and the LA- Pasadena via Short line were converted to one man service using 5050 cars on October 22, 1950. The last line to be converted to one-man operation was the Hollywood Blvd. (via Subway) line which changed on Jan. 14, 1951. The Watts Local line and the LA-Monrovia-Glendora line continued to operate using two man cars (the unrebuilt 732-759 and 5050's). Car 5050 is shown here inbound on the Santa Monica Blvd. local line at Highland Ave. in late 1950. *(Jim Buckley)*

Car 698 was rebuilt at the PE Torrance Shop to No. 5051 in the late summer of 1949, and is shown here on Jan. 2, 1950 (New Year's Day that year) returning from Pasadena on the Northern District four tracks at El Sereno. The distinctive lattice line structure was purchased from the Visalia Electric in 1929. *(Ken Douglas)*

Car 5056 (the former 693) is shown on an outbound Hollywood Blvd. train switching off of Hill Street on to private right of way leading to one of the Hill Street tunnels. Two reminders that the narrow gauge Los Angeles Railway had shared Hill Street with the PE are seen with the third (narrow) rail in the street and the overhead sign in the foreground. The narrow gauge cars had been gone about four years when this photo was taken on September 4, 1950. *(Ken Douglas)*

EFFECTIVE JULY 25, 1943

TIME
TABLE **3**

PACIFIC ELECTRIC RAIL LINES MOTOR COACH

RAIL AND MOTOR COACH

LOS ANGELES STATIONS
Main St. Station, 610 So. Main St.
Subway Terminal, 423 South Hill St.
Telephone TUcker 7272

LOS ANGELES LOCAL LINES

Hollywood Boulevard Line

Santa Monica Boulevard Line

Western-Franklin Motor Coach Line

Venice Blvd.-San Vicente Blvd. Line

Echo Park Avenue Line

Sierra Vista-Watts Line

Emery Park Motor Coach Line

Sunday schedules will be operated on New Year's Day, Memorial Day, Fourth of July, Labor Day, Thanksgiving Day and Christmas Day.

Subject to Change Without Notice

Schedule 3-20   10M—7-14-43

H. O. MARLER
Passenger Traffic Manager
Los Angeles

Heavy traffic and the capacity to handle it was evident at the Watts Station stop in July 1952, as a three car inbound Watts Local pulls up to the station. Soon the train will leave the first stop inbound to Los Angeles with car 5085 leading.
(William C. Janssen)

The afternoon rush is underway as cars 5065 and 5069 in train run outbound on the Venice Blvd. local line on August 2, 1950. This stretch of double track was shared by local cars and Venice Short line interurbans. Traffic was so heavy that two special passing tracks were used so that VSL trains could pass locals.
(Jim Buckley)

When the Watts Local Line and the Sierra Vista Local Line were separated on October 22, 1950 both routes were changed from their Main Street route and ran into the terminal at the rear of Main Street Station via San Pedro Street. 5094 and train are shown at the bottom of the viaduct leading from the station and about to turn right onto San Pedro Street outbound to Watts in September, 1952. By this time, the Sierra Vista line had been converted to bus *(William C. Janssen)*

After the Venice Blvd.-San Vicente line was converted to bus on October 1, 1950, a franchise run continued to operate over the line on weekdays. On the day before this operation was abandoned, Car 5108 is seen on the crossover at Vineyard on December 27, 1950. Car 5108 entered service on August 11, 1950 and was the former 641 *(Ken Douglas)*

PE 5110 was inbound from Van Nuys on the Subway-Van Nuys line passing the North Hollywood substation on October 12, 1952. The 5110 entered service on August 17, 1950 and was the former 639. PE 5011 is a fantrip car sitting on the substation siding. *(Ken Douglas)*

The Venice Short Line franchise car, PE 5112, has just returned from a trip over the Echo Park Ave. line and is southbound out of the northern Hill Street tunnel on the last day before service was abandoned, December 27, 1950. Car 5112 entered service 8/24/50, and was the former 637. *(Ken Douglas)*

Car 5112 was also used on other Western District lines. Here it is shown as the rear car of a Subway-Hollywood Blvd. train right in the middle of Hollywood in September, 1952. The train is crossing Highland Ave. and the overhead wires of the Van Nuys line can be seen over this street. No. 5112 was later moved to the Southern District for Watts service. The car is now preserved at the Orange Empire Railway Museum in Perris, Calif. *(William C. Janssen)*

On July 26, 1953 a fantrip was chartered over many of the remaining Western District lines of the PE, including the Santa Monica Air Line. Car 5116 assigned to the daily run to Santa Monica over the Air line is stored on a siding in Santa Monica, while the charter car, No. 5111 passes by. Both cars were also used on the Watts Local Line and both would remain in service until 1959. *(Ray Ballash)*

Car 5125 is shown having just turned off 9th St. onto the private right of way. At this point, the two tracks become four, and the car will take the switch to the local track on its outbound run to Amoco and the junction with the Santa Monica Air Line. This spot was unofficially known as "Oscar's Junction" (for Oscar Smith, the PE president). This is the last day of service for the Air Line, September 26, 1953. In the background and to the right, tracks can be seen leading to the 8th Street freight yard. *(Ray Ballash)*

Car 5125 is shown at Sentous yard stopped to pick up a railfan passenger while running as a charter over the Santa Monica Air Line on September 26, 1953. The daily run to Santa Monica over the air line had ceased on September 10th, but a short remnant running in Los Angeles to 11th St. continued to operate until this day, when passenger service over the whole line was abandoned. As all other passenger service had been sold to Metropolitan Coach Lines on October 1st, this was the very last PE passenger service to be operated. Note the Ringling Bros., Barnum & Bailey circus train stored on the siding behind the PE car. *(Ray Ballash)*

Another three car Watts Local is shown on the Southern District four tracks at Florence Ave. Comprised of cars 5128, 5124 and 5117, the first car will cut off the train at Amoco Junction for the daily franchise run over the Santa Monica Air Line, while the remaining two cars will continue on in service over the Watts Local Line on September 4, 1953. *(Ray Ballash)*

Car 5130 is passing Echo Park Lake on May 30, 1953 inbound on the Hollywood Blvd. Line. Soon the car will pass down the ramp and into the Subway portal for the short run into the Subway Terminal. *(Ray Ballash)*

At the extreme western end of the Subway-Hollywood Blvd.-Beverly Hills Line, Car 5131 is seen on September 25, 1954. The car has changed ends just past the Beverly Hills station and will soon start on an inbound trip to downtown. The service is being operated by Metro Coach Lines, and this is the last day of rail service on the line *(Ray Ballash)*

Car 5132, the former 617 entered service on May 23, 1950. Shown here in May, 1953 while running outbound on the Hollywood Blvd. line in front of the famous Grauman's Chinese Theatre. *(Emery Gulash)*

The Burbank Station yard was the end of the Glendale-Burbank line after November, 1949 when the line was cut back to this point. A new track arrangement made it much easier for cars to enter and leave the terminal. Most service over the lines to Glendale and North Glendale were operated by the 30 PCC cars, but 5050s were also required (13 being assigned in 1954). Car 5137, the former 612 is shown at Burbank on Feb. 28, 1954 heading a three car train which operated as a rush hour limited to downtown. PCC cars 5017 and 5022 can also be seen in this view. *(Ray Ballash)*

Car 5138 is shown operating inbound on the Subway-Hollywood Blvd.- Beverly Hills line on September 25, 1954. The car has just entered the private right of way passing the Toluca Substation on the left, and the Toluca storage yard on the right. In a few seconds, the car will enter the subway tunnel leading to the terminal. The car is being operated by Metro Coach and this is the last day of service for this rail line. *(Ray Ballash)*

Car 5140, the former 609 is shown running inbound on the Subway- Hollywood Blvd.-Beverly Hills line on August 28, 1954. The car is passing the Toluca substation on the left and the Toluca six track storage yard on the right. In a few seconds, the car will enter the subway portal for the one-mile run to Subway Terminal. *(Ray Ballash)*

The outer end of the Hollywood Blvd. line ran on several stretches of private right of way. On a typical (of Southern California) spring morning with fog and low clouds, car 5141 is shown inbound at North Spaulding on April 24, 1954. Car 5141 was rebuilt from the 608 on June 17, 1950. By September 26th, when the line will be abandoned, the car will be out of use. *(Ray Ballash)*

Cars 5143 and 5163 pass on the right of way at at spot known as Gardner Junction. By the date of this photo on April 24, 1954 the site contained only this crossover, where many cars turned back for the run to downtown Los Angeles. In earlier years, an actual junction was located at this point where a single track line to Laurel Canyon branched from the mainline. *(Ray Ballash)*

Hollywood Junction was the point where a connection was made at Sunset Blvd. and Bonnie Brae St. with the tracks of the Glendale-Burbank Line via a short section of track on Park Blvd. This connection was made so that cars operating on the Santa Monica Blvd., Hollywood Blvd. and San Fernando Valley could enter the subway. On May 30, 1953, Car 5144 is about to turn off Sunset onto Park Ave. while operating inbound on the Santa Monica Blvd. line. *(Ray Ballash)*

Car 5145, the former 604 is shown on September 25, 1954 operating inbound on the Hollywood Blvd. line on the last day of service. The car has just turned off Sunset Blvd. and will shortly turn onto the rails of the Glendale-Burbank line. *(Ray Ballash)*

Park Junction was the spot where the lines from Hollywood connected with the Glendale-Burbank line to gain access to Subway Terminal. This connecting link was built in 1926. On September 25, 1954, car 5147 and 5129 pass at the junction, which was located in front of the Angelus Temple. *(Ray Ballash)*

Car 5148, the former 601 is shown here on November 9, 1953 outbound on Hollywood Blvd. The service is now being operated by Metropolitan Coach Lines which took over the passenger service of PE on October 1st of that year. *(Emery Gulash)*

Because of the heavy traffic, PE ran multicar trains on the Hollywood Blvd. line, but with the conversion to one man-operation in January, 1951 single cars running on more frequent headways became the norm. Cars 5149 and 5146 pass on Hollywood Blvd. at Cosmos Street almost at the center of Hollywood on August 28, 1954. *(Ray Ballash)*

Past the downtown area of Hollywood, PE cars turned southwest at La Brea and operated over some very narrow streets to reach private right of way. Car 5150, the former 700 is shown here at Hawthorne outbound on April 24, 1954. *(Ray Ballash)*

As can be noted, most of the Hollywood service had to operate on city streets once it left the Subway Car 5153 (the former 703) is shown here running outbound on Sunset Blvd. at Virgil Ave. on August 28, 1954. *(Ray Ballash)*

Running on the Glendale-Burbank Line, cars 5158 and 5163 are shown outbound on June 14, 1955. The train has just passed under Sunset Blvd. and in the background is the Angelus Temple, where Park Junction was located. By this time, the service was operated by Metropolitan Coach Lines (as can be noted from the colors of the bus running on Sunset) and the line has only a few more days to operate. Rail service on the Glendale-Burbank line will cease on June 19th. *(Ray Ballash)*

Car 5177 is shown here having just arrived at North Hollywood. A good load of passengers will board the northbound car which is headed for Van Nuys in June, 1952. 5177 is the former 727, and was among the last of the 5050's to be rebuilt in 1951. *(Emery Gulash)*

As the Pacific Electric and Metropolitan Coach Lines abandoned rail service from 1951 to 1955, the 5050's used to operate these lines were placed into dead storage at various locations around the system including the Torrance Shops, West Hollywood Car House, Toluca Yard and the subway and on unused freight spurs in the 8th Street freight yard, just south of the downtown area of Los Angeles. This view, taken on November 5, 1954 shows a line of cars in storage. Across the yard next to the freight house can be seen another line of 5050's. Eight of these cars were sold to Portland, Ore. for further service and fifteen were assigned to the Watts Local Line (only ten remained in service at the end in 1959). The rest were hauled away for scrap in 1956, hardly broken in from their rehabilitation only a few years earlier. *(Ira Swett)*

As a result of California Public Utilities Commission recommendations after the ill-fated experiment of 1936-1940 where the Glendale-Burbank line was partially operated by motor coaches, the PE bought from Pullman in 1940 thirty double ended PCC cars. Some were slated to run on the Venice Short line, but rough track caused the lines to be concentrated on the Glendale-Burbank line where they ran until 1955 when the line was converted to bus. Cars 5001 and 5027 are shown outbound on the Fletcher Drive Bridge on the Glendale-Burbank line in March, 1948. *(Ken Douglas)*

At the terminal yard in Burbank, PCCs 5004 and 5026 are in the company of a 5050 on May 1, 1954. Note that the destination sign on 5004 has been turned to "Sierra Vista", a northern district line where the PCCs never ran. *(Ray Ballash)*

The PE PCC cars were capable of multiple unit operation, and often were run in trains. Three units were the maximum length of these trains, but views of more than two of them operating together are uncommon. Nos. 5006 and 5011 are shown operating northbound (outbound) at Arden Junction on June 10, 1955. Some trains continue north at this point to a terminal at North Glendale, but most will turn northwest to continue to Burbank. *(Ray Ballash)*

PE 5008 was photographed at the 11th and Hill crossover of the Hollywood Blvd. line on January 2, 1950. The PCCs were only operated on this line on New Year's Day (or the next day if New Year's Day was on a Sunday, as it was in 1950). *(Ken Douglas)*

The Glendale-Burbank line (now operated by Metropolitan Coach Lines) has four more days to operate as a rail line when PCC 5012 was photographed at the Burbank terminal on June 16, 1955. Shown while changing ends after just arriving from downtown Los Angeles, the car will soon return as an inbound train. The "June Gloom" overcast skies add their own touch to the ending of the rail service. *(Emery Gulash)*

PCC Cars 5018 and 5025 were photographed on May 19, 1949 inbound to the Subway Terminal in Burbank. When built, PE's PCC cars were operated by two men, a motorman and conductor. In January, 1950 the Glendale-Burbank line was converted to one-man operation. *(Emery Gulash)*

The Glendale-Burbank line used considerable stretches of private right of way, and included several large bridges. One bridge crossed the Los Angeles River, and is seen here on May 20, 1949, when PCC 5024 is seen running inbound to Los Angeles. *(Emery Gulash)*

PE 5021 was being operated by Metro Coach Lines when photographed in Glendale in May, 1953 waiting for a traffic light. *(Emery Gulash)*

On September 26, 1954, the last day of rail service for the Subway-Hollywood Blvd.-Beverly Hills line, car 5024 was chartered and ran over the line. Shown here in the heart of Hollywood at Hollywood Blvd. and Vine St. the car poses for photographers. The cars were used in passenger service over this line on New Years Day, and occasionally could be seen running to and from the West Hollywood Car House for servicing. *(Ray Ballash)*

The oldest interurban cars left on the PE in passenger service after World War Two were the 950's. Built by St. Louis in 1907 for predecessor Los Angeles-Pacific the cars were used to Pasadena until the delivery of the 1100's in 1924 and then were moved back to the Western District where they were primarily used on the Venice Short Line and the Santa Monica via Beverly Hills routes. A three car train, comprised of cars 952, 995 and 986 are shown outbound on Venice Blvd. On August 2, 1950. In a little over a month, the line will be converted to bus and the cars retired. Abandonment of the Santa Monica via Beverly Hills line in 1940 allowed many of the 950's to be scrapped. World War Two caused the remaining 31 cars to be refurbished at the Torrance Shops. By war's end however, the cars were run down and in need of replacement. The class was often cited as examples of obsolete vehicles in need of replacement when PE was trying to abandon rail service. Car 954 is shown running inbound to Los Angeles over the fine right of way of the Venice Short Line between Culver City and Vineyard on May 21, 1949. *(Emery Gulash)*

PE 957 is shown on September 28, 1949 leading a four car train outbound on the Venice Short Line. Four car operation of the 950's was uncommon for regular service, but did occur on Monday through Fridays during the school year to and from Venice High School in the mornings and afternoons. A crew of nine men was required to prevent vandalism. *(Ken Douglas)*

An outbound Venice Short Line train, comprised of cars 960 and 954 are seen at Venice & Vermont, crossing the Los Angeles Transit Line "V" line. An inbound Venice Blvd.-Hollywood Blvd. local car will shortly pass the train of big wooden cars on August 2, 1950. The 950's were last used in service on Friday, September 15, 1950, and with the abandonment of the Venice Short line on September 17th the 950's were out of a job. They were officially retired on November 9, 1950. After a period of storage, the cars were sold for scrap and sent to Terminal Island. *(Jim Buckley)*

Car 962 and train are slowing for the junction at Vineyard on September 13, 1949 on an inbound Venice Short Line train. In a few minutes, the cars will enter street trackage on Venice Blvd. for the final portion of the trip to the Hill Street Terminal. *(Henry Stange)*

PE 965 is shown inbound on the Venice Short Line on the Trolleyway private right of way in Ocean Park on November 12, 1949. *(Ken Douglas)*

A fantrip was run on Feb. 12, 1950 operating over many lines on the Western District. PE 966 is shown alongside PE 106 at the end of the Echo Park Ave. line at Echo Park Ave. and Cerro Gordo. Incongruity is the element here, a fan trip speciality. The interurban car is at the end of a local streetcar line served by the smallest passenger cars then operating on the PE. *(Ken Douglas)*

At Vineyard, the Venice Short Line turned off the congested streets of Los Angeles and entered the long stretch of private right of way leading to the beach at Venice. Car 990 is shown in April, 1949 while heading a two car train outbound on the Venice Short Line at Vineyard. *(Henry Stange)*

PE 990 is shown leading a deadhead train leaving the Hill St. surface tracks onto Hill Street on September 4, 1950. Limited storage at the Hill St. terminal caused many interurban and local cars to be moved to Vineyard for mid-day storage. *(Ken Douglas)*

During the off-peak hours, cars for the Vineyard-Hollywood Blvd. local line and the Venice Short Line were stored some distance from downtown at Vineyard Junction and West Hollywood Car House, due to limited space at the Hill Street Surface Station. Here PE 993 and train are being readied for an inbound deadhead trip to the Hill Street Station on September 13, 1949. Since the cars will be reversed to head outbound on the Venice Short line to Santa Monica, the destination signs will likely be changed at the Hill Street Station. *(Jim Konas)*

PE 999 is shown on November 12, 1949 at the Ocean Park Carhouse. The 999 was converted by its original owner, the Los Angeles-Pacific to a deluxe car, the *El Viento*. During its conversion, the original three window front was converted to a five window front with curved glass corner windows. The car was later converted to a standard interurban coach and assigned the number 999. *(Ken Douglas)*

The 1000's were built by Jewett in 1913 and were comprised of two groups of cars. Nos. 1000-1044 were constructed for the PE. Nos. 1050-1057 were built for the Peninsular Ry., an SP subsidiary operating out of San Jose, and came to Los Angeles in the 1930's. After a period of storage at the Torrance Shops, the Peninsular cars were refurbished and put into service on the Alhambra-Temple City line. When that line was converted to motor coach in early 1941, they were pooled with the other 1000s. An example of the original group, PE 1002 and two others are shown inbound on the Venice Short Line on Venice Blvd. in Los Angeles on May 20, 1949. *(Emery Gulash)*

PE 1002 is shown at the West Hollywood Carhouse on January 15, 1950, ready for another trip on the Venice Short Line. Sister car 1001 was converted to a rail grinder and renumbered 00199. Fortunately, this car was saved and has been restored at the Orange Empire Railway Museum. *(Ken Douglas)*

With delivery of steel cars (the 1200s and 1100s) in 1915, 1921, 1924 and 1929, the tens were eclipsed as first line cars on the PE. Most of them were then assigned to the Southern District in later years. During World War Two, when the 1100 and 1200-series were modernized, the cars saw extensive service again on the Northern District. In 1942, the tens were modernized at Torrance. This modernization consisting of having the toilets removed, seats added, 1200- volt features blocked off, new lighting and paint. PE 1009 is shown running eastbound on the Long Beach-San Pedro line between East Wilmington Junction and Pioneer Junction on December 29, 1948. This line will be converted to bus in a few days, on January 2, 1949. *(Ken Douglas)*

PE 1009 is shown again a few miles west of the previous photo on the Long Beach-San Pedro Line at Wilmington Station on December 29, 1949. This station was located on the main line of the Los Angeles-San Pedro Line. *(Ken Douglas)*

PE 1012 is turning off Ocean Blvd. in Long Beach, westbound on the Long Beach-San Pedro line. This is near Morgan Ave. storage yard. This line was the last interurban line on the PE which did not serve Los Angeles. This view was taken on December 29, 1949, and the line would be converted to motor coach operation in a few days. The tracks and overhead would remain for freight service. *(Ken Douglas)*

At East Wilmington Junction, the Long Beach-San Pedro line joined the Los Angeles-San Pedro line. PE 1012 has just cleared a southbound box motor and is proceeding onto the San Pedro mainline westbound in this view taken on December 29, 1949. *(Ken Douglas)*

With the conversion of the Long Beach-San Pedro line to motor coach, PE 1012 was sent to the Western District for use on the Venice Short Line. PE 1012 and 1002 are shown running inbound on Venice Blvd. in the afternoon on August 2, 1950. *(Jim Buckley)*

The horse racing season at Santa Anita race track was a big traffic generator for the PE, and many trains were run over the Monrovia-Glendora line to the racetrack. A long siding at this point held cars for the the rush back to Los Angeles after the last race. Car 1003 is shown at the end of a string of tens on this siding, which was in the city of Arcadia, in January, 1949. *(Ira Swett)*

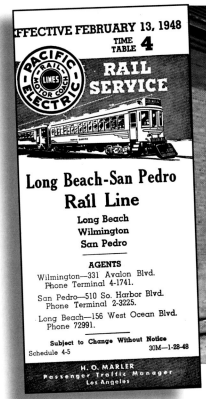

After intensive use during WWII, declining traffic levels reduced the need for the tens. A few were sent to the Western District for use on the Venice Short Line. Some were used on the San Pedro-Long Beach line, but most were stored at Torrance, until some special need arose such as the racing season at Santa Anita. Although larger and more modern that the 950's, the tens could only supplement the older cars on the Western District, because their size created storage problems in the cramped Hill St. Station. Clearances (and a lack of signal trips) kept them from running into the Subway. Much of the time in the late 1940's cars of the 1000-series were in storage at West Hollywood and Torrance. PE 1013 is shown at West Hollywood Carhouse on September 13, 1949. (*Jim Konas*)

PE 1016 is also shown at the West Hollywood Carhouse on September 13, 1949. The headsign has been turned to a destination on the Southern District where the tens were not regularly used after June 9, 1940 (rails between Newport and Balboa were torn up in 1941). (*Henry Stange*)

Three car trains of 1000's were usually the longest that could be seen on the Venice Short Line. In this view, taken on August 2, 1950, Nos. 1019, 1017 and 1013 are running outbound on Hill Street at Pico in the morning. *(Jim Buckley)*

PE 1036 has operated its last mile in revenue service. The car has been stored at the Torrance Shop and will soon be taken inside to be stripped of parts and then burned. Note that the car is stored on a track without overhead. It will be necessary for the car to be pulled out by the shop switcher using a long chain. Other tens and wooden box motors await a similar fate in this view taken on September 12, 1949. *(Henry Stange)*

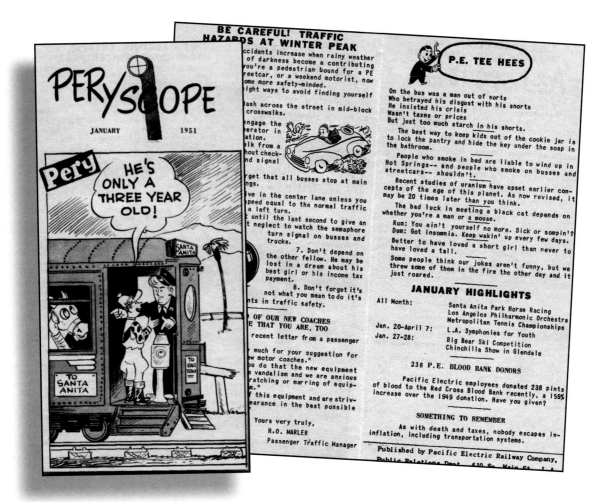

After World War Two, the tens were not often seen on the elevated tracks of Main Street Station in downtown Los Angeles. They did run from here during the winter months for Santa Anita racetrack service (and to the Tournament of Roses on New Years) and on the once a day Santa Monica Air Line run. Car 1044 is shown here switching in the station on September 10, 1949. *(Henry Stange)*

PE 1052, the former Peninsular Ry. 107 is shown here in March, 1948 at the Ocean Park Carhouse. The car would remain available for service on this line until it was converted to motor coach on September 17, 1950. The car was sold for scrap and sent to Terminal Island to be burned the following year.
(Emery Gulash)

Until they were replaced with Hollywood Cars, a ten was often assigned to the daily run on the Santa Monica Air Line. PE 1056 (former Peninsular Ry. 111) is shown at Macy Street Yard while laying over for this assignment. In the afternoon, the car will deadhead to Main Street Station and operate outbound over the Southern District four tracks where it will switch to the Air Line and run to Santa Monica. Usually a one car operation, the run could blossom to three cars when the Los Angeles Railway/Transit Lines were hit with a labor strike.
(Ken Douglas)

The PE 1100-series were comprised of fifty cars built by Standard Steel Car Co. in 1924. Numbered 1100-1149, the cars were designed to be used on the 600-volt lines of the Northern District, where heavy grades were a factor. The cars resembled the 1200-series, but had double side doors, a lower gear ratio and smaller wheels so were basically a heavy suburban car. PE 1100, the first car of the class is shown on October 15, 1950 crossing the Santa Ana River Bridge just west of the City of Santa Ana on the Santa Ana line (on the Southern District). Passenger service over this portion of the line had ended on June 2nd, and this is a fantrip car. The 1100 class were almost always used on the Northern District during the post-WWII period. *(Ken Douglas)*

The use of the 1100s was reduced in early October 1950, when the Pasadena via Oak Knoll and the Sierra Madre lines were converted to bus operation. Later that month, operation of Pasadena Short Line trains was changed to 5050 type cars, operated with one-man. Many cars were put in storage, but a few continued in use on the Monrovia-Glendora Line until March 19, 1951 when Hollywood cars (752 and 5050 types running two-man) replaced them. Time was running out on the 1100s when this shot was taken of 1101 and train at El Molino in February, 1951. *(Ira Swett)*

PE 1102 is shown inbound on the Glendora Line at El Molino. The tracks coming in from the left belong to the Pasadena via Oak Knoll line. The Northern District four tracks ended just west of this view taken on December 29, 1949. *(Ken Douglas)*

The Northern District four track right of way was well maintained even after PE had decided to abandon all service over these tracks. On September 11, 1949, car 1108 was shot while running inbound on the Pasadena via Oak Knoll line to Los Angeles. *(Henry Stange)*

Car No. 1109 has changed ends at the Glendora station, and the crew is taking a bit of spot time before making another inbound run to Los Angeles. *(Jim Konas)*

The 1100s (or any other steel interurban car) were never used in regular service on the Western District. However on special occasions and fantrips they were run on this District. No. 1111 and PCC 5017 are shown at the Burbank station in 1951. *(Fred Matthews)*

Runs on both the northbound Pasadena lines terminated at the Pasadena Carhouse on North Fair Oaks. After unloading passengers, car 1112 is turning into the carhouse in March, 1949. Note the conductor leading out the side window flagging the turn into the barn. *(Emery Gulash)*

PE 1114 is running outbound on the Monrovia-Glendora line at Arcadia. The siding on the right is for storage of Santa Anita horse racing specials, but by the date of this photo on May 20, 1949 the season is over for another year. *(Emery Gulash)*

Many runs on the Monrovia-Glendora line ended at Monrovia where the PE tracks ran down the middle of a street in front of the station. Car 1116 is the second car of a two car train outbound in this view taken in February, 1951. In less than a month, Hollywood cars will take over the operation of this line and on September 30th, passenger service will be converted to bus operation. *(Ira Swett)*

PE 1119 heels to the curve as it turns off the viaduct at the rear of Main Street Station on a northbound run to Pasadena via Oak Knoll. It is early morning and a single car will suffice for this trip, while inbound trains will consist of several cars coupled together to bring morning commuters into Los Angeles on this view taken on September 10, 1949. *(Henry Stange)*

As has been mentioned elsewhere, from 1949-51 most of the Hollywood cars were rebuilt for one-man service. This created a shortage of cars for local service, so in July, 1949 PE 1100, 1102, 1106, 1107, 1107, 1113, 1116, 1119 and 1128 were equipped with farebox holders for service on the Sierra Vista-Watts line. The farebox had to be mounted on the rear platform, since fares on the interurbans were usually collected by the conductor at the passenger's seat. Car 1122 heads a southbound train to Watts at Florence Ave. on the Southern District four tracks on May 3, 1950. *(Ken Douglas)*

PE 1123 was photographed in March, 1948 while approaching Echandia Junction just east of the Macy Street Carhouse. The car is operating on the Pasadena via Oak Knoll line. Note that when the car was repainted, the striping below the windows was left off. *(Ken Douglas)*

On October 13, 1948, car 1124 was photographed running outbound on the Monrovia-Glendora line, on the west end of the San Gabriel River bridge. *(Ken Douglas)*

Pasadena Short Line trains ran in the middle of Fair Oaks Ave. through downtown Pasadena to the four track right of way along Huntington Drive at Oneonta Junction. At the South end, the line was on private right of way. Car 1132 heads an inbound special returning from Pasadena just north of Oneonta Junction on January 2, 1950. *(Ken Douglas)*

PE 1136, running inbound on a Pasadena via Oak Knoll train passes Macy Street Yard and Carhouse on August 2, 1950. The last 1100s were taken out of service on March 21, 1951 and stored. They were sold for further service to Argentina, where they ran until the early 1970s. A few were demotorized and sold to Paraguay, where they ran behind wood burning steam locomotives! *(Jim Buckley)*

Pasadena Short Line trains ran on Fair Oaks Ave. from downtown Pasadena to the four track right of way along Huntington Drive at Oneonta Junction. Car 1139 is shown running inbound on this important street in this view taken in March, 1949. *(Emery Gulash)*

The Tournament of Roses parade and football game brought much business to the PE on New Year's Day. PE 1146 is heading an inbound special returning from Pasadena on January 2, 1950 on the Oak Knoll line private right of way near the Huntington Hotel, which can be seen in the background. *(Ken Douglas)*

The 1200s were considered PE's finest interurbans from their introduction in 1915 until they were scrapped in 1951. The class actually consisted of four different types of cars. Nos. 1200-1221 were built by Pressed Steel in 1915 and equipped by General Electric. Built for 600/1200 volt lines, the cars were placed into service on the San Bernardino line. After a time, they saw use on most Northern and Southern District lines. Built with lavatories, cars 1200- 1215 were modernized in 1941-42 and had this feature removed, being equipped with additional seating. After this modernization, cars 1220-1216 resembled the 1222-1245 type. The first twelve, car 1200 is shown at the end of the Baldwin Park line at Maine Avenue on October 30, 1949. *(Ken Douglas)*

PE 1205 is shown outbound on the Baldwin Park line just east of Valley Junction on March 13, 1949. The trolley sectionalizing can be seen in the overhead wire where the voltage changed from 600 to 1200-volts on the eastbound trip. The motorman would actuate a commutation switch in the cab which changed the cars electric circuits to accommodate the change in voltage and coast through the break with power off. *(Ken Douglas)*

By May, 1949 when this shot of PE 1205 heading a two car train, use of the 1200s on the Long Beach Line was becoming uncommon as most runs were handled by Blimps. The cars are ready to depart the 6th & Main St. Station on May 8, 1949 for a southbound trip to Long Beach. Rising above the station platforms is the PE Building, nerve center of the Red Car System.
(Ken Douglas)

In 1939, cars 1216-1221 were modernized to rehabilitate service on the San Bernardino Line. New seats, lighting, faired destination signs and a spectacular paint job marked this rebuilding. The cars had little chance to prove themselves however, as the San Bernardino line was converted to buses in 1941. Thereafter the cars, known as "Butterfly Twelves" were used in pool service with the other 1200s. PE 1216 is shown inbound at El Monte on the Baldwin Park line on October 31, 1948. In the rebuilding of 1939, the cars kept their lavatories and the oval window marking this facility can be seen on the side near the front.
(Ken Douglas)

PE 1218 and 1216 were photographed on a weekday outbound Newport Beach Express on the four track viaduct over Manchester Ave. on May 3, 1950. Most service on the Newport line by this time was by motor coach, but several runs a day were run over the rails to Newport. The second car will be cut off at Seal Beach. *(Ken Douglas)*

The very last day for operation of the Newport Beach Express was June 30, 1950. Cars 1216 and 1218 are shown entering Main Street Station from the viaduct with the deadhead equipment for the very last scheduled passenger train on the line. Because the Newport line did not have the trolley wire greased like most lines running passenger service, the PE required that cars used here (and on other freight lines) had to use trolley wheels which can be seen on the cars. *(Ken Douglas)*

PE 1220 is shown on September 10, 1949 at the Newport Beach station shortly after arriving from Los Angeles. Normal procedure was for the car to be stored overnight and used for the first inbound train in the morning. *(Henry Stange)*

On the Baldwin Park line, some runs during rush hours did not run all the way through to the terminal, and were cut back at El Monte. Car 1221 was photographed in March, 1948 while outbound on the Baldwin Park line at State Street.
(Ken Douglas)

PE 1221 is seen again inbound at Valley Junction on a deadhead move into Los Angeles for use as a Santa Anita Race Track special on December 13, 1949. The reinforced concrete building in the background is the Valley Junction substation.
(Ken Douglas)

The second group of PE 1200s were nos. 1222-1245 (and trailers 1246- 1251) which were built by Pullman in 1921 to reequip the Long Beach line. The cars were geared slightly lower than 1201-1221 and had no lavatories, but were otherwise similar to the earlier cars and could operate in multiple with them. Car 1236 is shown at Macy Street Yard in August 1949.
(Fred Matthews)

PE 1237 will shortly deadhead inbound to Los Angles on August 2, 1950 from the Macy Street Carhouse. The car will be used for a regular run on the Baldwin Park line. Like 1200-1215, cars 1222-1245 were partially modernized just prior to World War Two. At that time they were given the paint scheme seen here. *(Jim Buckley)*

In early fall, Los Angeles held their annual County Fair near Pomona. PE ran trains to the fair over the San Bernardino line. PE 1239 is shown with a two car County Fair special at La Verne. This was the junction of the branch which used to go into downtown Pomona from the San Bernardino mainline. The conductor has just thrown the switch for the train to go onto the branch on October 1, 1950. *(Ken Douglas)*

The third group of PE 1200s were trailers 1246-1251, which were built with 1222-1245 to operate on the Long Beach line. These trailers (called "sleds" by PE crews) were not heavily used, and four (PE 1242-1245) were given motors in 1946-47 to improve utilization. Car 1243, one of the converted trailers is seen here on October 15, 1950 on the Rialto Packing House spur. This spur was all that was left of the PE line from Rialto to Riverside. *(Ken Douglas)*

The fourth group of PE 1200s were nos. 1252-1262. These cars were built by Pullman in 1913 for SP electric lines in Oregon. They were sent to the PE after abandonment of the Oregon lines. Nos. 1252-1257 entered service in 1929 as Parlor Cars, while 1258-1262 followed soon after as coaches. The parlor cars were changed to coaches in 1937, and thereafter all "Portland Twelves" operated in pool service with the rest of the 1200s. The cars were equipped with lavatories, but these were removed in a modernization program just before World War Two and replaced with additional seats. The cars were noticably different from the other 1200s by their use of round end windows and leaded glass upper sash in the side windows. Car 1252 is shown with a three car Tournament of Roses Special on January 2, 1950. During the later years of PE passenger service, this was the only time cars were operated through the concourse at the 6th and Main Street Station. Usually cars used the elevated tracks at the rear of the station and buses used the concourse. The concourse tracks connected with the elevated tracks at the rear and descended to street level at Main Street. *(Ken Douglas)*

PE 1256 is heading an inbound Tournament of Roses special returning from Pasadena on January 2, 1950 on the Pasadena Short line just north of Oneonta Junction. *(Ken Douglas)*

The leaded glass upper sash in the side windows can be seen to good effect in this view of PE 1257 taken on February 10, 1950 at the Macy Street Yards. *(Fred Matthews)*

PE 1259 is shown inbound at Macy Street Yard while running on the Baldwin Park Line on August 2, 1950. *(Jim Buckley)*

Because of the 1200 volt operation, the Twelves were required to run on the Baldwin Park Line as they were the only passenger cars capable of operating at this voltage after World War Two. PE 1260 and train are shown running inbound on San Pedro Street at Boyd on August 4, 1950. The cars will continue south on San Pedro and turn onto the viaduct into the 6th and Main Street Station just south of Sixth Street. *(Ken Douglas)*

A two car train, headed by PE 1260 is shown at the Pomona Fairgrounds on October 1, 1950. During the Los Angeles County Fair, the PE ran specials to the Fairgrounds. Beyond Baldwin Park, these runs were operating on trackage that was normally freight only. The year 1950 was to be the last for the specials to run to the fairgounds. Note the spoke pilot on the 1260, unique to the former Portland 1200s. *(Ken Douglas)*

PE 1261 is shown on the Seventh St. Surface Tracks on September 11, 1949. These tracks were located under the Main Street Station elevated tracks, used for car storage and by box motors for loading and unloading. Most of the tracks here were abandoned in the summer of 1950. After that time, cars were stored at 8th St. Yard and Macy Street. Later in the day, this car will be used for a Catalina Boat Train Special to the harbor. *(Emery Gulash)*

One additional Portland car was purchased and used by the PE. Former SP trailer 477 was rebuilt at Torrance in 1929 as a business car. Special low trolley bases were installed, so the car could operate in the Subway, the only large PE steel interurban car to be allowed in that facility. The car could be operated in MU with the other 1200s. During the summer months after World War Two, the car ran as the *Commodore* to Newport Beach, the only time the car was used by the public. The car was available for charter however, and was used on fan trips. The car is shown here on June 2, 1951 at Pomona on the San Bernardino line on a fantrip. *(Jim Konas)*

Two combination baggage-passenger cars were built by Pressed Steel in 1915 to operate with 1200-1221. Numbered 1370-1371, the cars were not only used on runs requiring baggage space, but also as regular passenger cars in the middle of trains. Steps at both ends allowed passengers to board by walking through the baggage compartment when necessary. Unlike the other 1200s, the combines were not modernized and ran to the end essentially as built. No. 1370 is shown at Macy Street Yard on September 10, 1949. *(Henry Stange)*

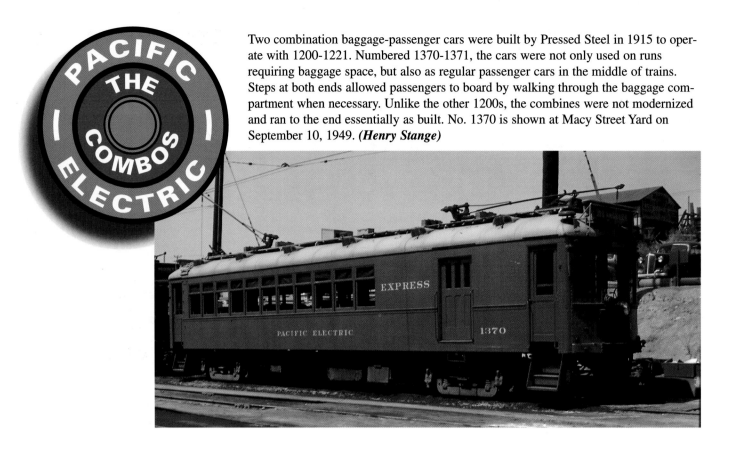

PE 1371 is shown outbound with a three car Tournament of Roses Special at the east end of State Street Yard. In later years, the combos which were built at the same time as the 1200s were not used extensively. However, all bets were off on New Years Day when almost any kind of equipment could be seen running to Pasadena. This view was taken on Jan. 1, 1949. *(Ken Douglas)*

Five Portland combos also came to the PE from the SP lines in Oregon, entering service in 1928. All were built by Pullman in 1913. The cars had their lavatories removed in 1942 and replaced with additional seats, but were otherwise not changed. PE 1372 is an example of one of these combos and is shown on December 28, 1949 leading a three car Santa Anita Race Track special at San Marino station. *(Ken Douglas)*

PE 1374 is shown at Macy Street Carhouse on September 19, 1948. Considering that the class 1200 cars and their corresponding 1370 combines were rarely used on the Catalina Specials by this date, it is more than probable that the roll sign was adjusted by the photographer. *(Ken Douglas)*

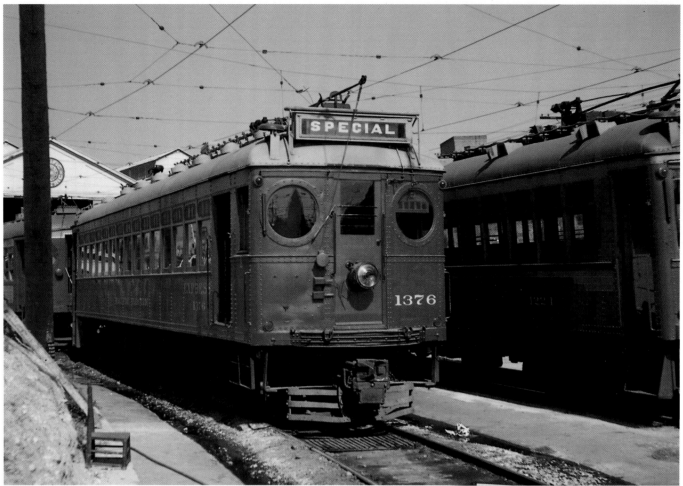

The highest numbered Portland combine was PE 1376, which is shown here at Macy Street Carhouse in August, 1949. With the abandonment of the Baldwin Park Line and two man operation on many of the other Northern District interurban lines, the 1200s and their combos were stored. In early 1951 all were sold for scrap and hauled to the Kaiser Steel Mill in Fontana for scrapping. *(Emery Gulash)*

EFFECTIVE MAY 29, 1950

TIME TABLE **8**

PACIFIC ELECTRIC

RAIL AND MOTOR COACH

LOS ANGELES TERMINAL
Main St. Station, 610 So. Main St.

LOS ANGELES-
EL MONTE-
BALDWIN PARK
RAIL LINE

LOS ANGELES-
POMONA VIA COVINA
MOTOR COACH LINE

LOS ANGELES-BALDWIN PARK-
COVINA-SAN DIMAS-
LA VERNE-POMONA

Subject to change without Notice

Schedule No. 8-31

H. O. MARLER
Passenger Traffic Manager
Los Angeles

THE NWP
HOT RODS & FORMER TRAILERS
BLIMPS

As traffic levels picked up during World War Two, the Southern Pacific sent to the PE in 1942 nineteen large cars formerly operated by the Northwestern Pacific Ry. in Northern California. The cars had been built by St. Louis in 1929 and 1930, and consisted of 12 motor cars and 7 trailers. After some modifications so that they could operate on the PE, the cars entered service as nos. 4500-4517. The trailers were considered too inflexible and in 1943 all were rebuilt as motor cars, using motor trucks and other equipment purchased from the U.S. Maritime Commission. Because of their large passenger capacity, the NWP cars were modernized at Torrance in 1946-47 and renumbered 300-318. Because of their large size, the cars were known as "Blimps". PE 306, the former 4507 is an example of the "Hot Rods" which were former NWP motor cars. Shown here in September, 1952, the car is about to turn off Ocean Blvd. in Long Beach north on American Ave. on an inbound run to Los Angeles. On the right, a PE White Model 798 bus can be seen running on the Huntington Park-Long Beach Line.*(William C. Janssen)*

Although the design of the ex-NWP "Blimps" was based on the SP cars operated on the East Bay electric lines, there were noticeable differences in window spacing, pilots, headlights and trolley bases. The former NWP motor cars were known as "Hot Rods" because of their higher gear ratio and were given preferential assignments. They were used so heavily that by 1958, when the Bellflower line was converted to bus, those remaining were retired. Fortunately, "Hot Rod" 314 has been preserved at the Orange Empire Railway Museum. PE 317 was photographed on September 10, 1949 at the Santa Ana Station ready for an inbound trip to Los Angeles. *(Henry Stange)*

After their rebuilding, the 300's were used on the remaining Southern District interurban lines, especially to Long Beach, San Pedro and Bellflower-Santa Ana. Most of the former trailers lasted to the end of interurban service in 1961. Car 300, former trailer 4514 is shown on December 29, 1949 while running inbound on the San Pedro Line. *(Ken Douglas)*

PE 318 is shown outbound on the Santa Ana line at Socorro. This is the end of double track just east of the junction with the main line at Watts. The concrete structure is the phone booth where the conductor has checked the train register to assure that all scheduled inbound cars which should be clear of the single track are indeed clear. The conductor has also contacted the dispatcher to determine if any train orders are required. The photo was taken in March, 1948. *(Ken Douglas)*

"Hot Rod" 318 is shown again at the Bellflower station on July 18, 1957 after passenger operations had been taken over by Metro Coach Lines. This was where passenger service ended on the Santa Ana line after being cut back in 1950. The rail service would operate on this line until May 25, 1958 when it was converted to motor coach by the Metropolitan Transit Authority. *(Edward S. Miller)*

In July and September, 1942 the U.S. Maritime Commission requisitioned 81 electric cars from the Southern Pacific Co. which had been made redundant with the abandonment of the SP Oakland-Alameda-Berkely operations (known as the Interurban Electric Ry.) in 1941. Sixty-one cars were sent to Los Angeles to be operated by the PE for service to Terminal Island shipyards. The cars were modified at Torrance Shops for PE service conditions and entered service in 1943 carrying their old SP-IER numbers and the U.S. Maritime Commission name on the letterboard. The USMC trains did not attract war workers in expected numbers, and in 1944 the PE purchased 30 cars to use on their lines that had experienced heavy traffic increases. After the war, PE purchased the remaining cars from the USMC and the coaches were numbered 4600-4647. As with the former NWP cars, the large capacity of these "Blimps" caused the PE to modernize them in 1946-48. After the rebuilding, the cars were numbered 400-437 and 450-459. The first SP "Blimp" to be rebuilt was the 400, shown here on August 8, 1949 at the 6th and Main Street Station. These cars will soon be used on the daily Catalina Special boat train. *(Ken Douglas)*

The SP cars had been built by American Car & Foundry and Pullman in 1911 and 1913. Until their rebuilding in 1946-48, they were much inferior to the other interurban cars operated by the PE but the advantages of their large capacity offset the lower speeds in the estimation of PE management. PE 401 is leading a three-car Santa Anita Race Track special at Harriman Road on the Northern District four tracks on December 31, 1949. *(Ken Douglas)*

Until the Main Street Station tracks were abandoned in the summer of 1950, cars were stored there in between runs to and from Main Street Station. A four car train headed by No. 411 is seen deadheading from the surface tracks over 7th Street on September 10, 1949. These tracks were only used in later years by PE for box motor runs and deadhead passenger car runs into the surface tracks, but a number of Los Angeles Transit Lines routes provided regular service on Seventh Street. *(Henry Stange)*

PE 432 is shown stored by the Watts substation across the tracks from the Watts Carhouse on November 10, 1953.
(Emery Gulash)

The great length of the PE Blimps is emphasized in this view of PE 419 unloading after arriving at San Pedro Station in September, 1952. Two of the PE 400's have been preserved, 418 at the Orange Empire Railway Museum and 435 (as MTA 1543) at Travel Town in Los Angeles.
(William C. Janssen)

One passenger service that used "Blimps" in later years that didn't appear in the public timetable was the train for shop workers that ran to the Torrance Shops for the benefit of PE employees. On October 10, 1949, car 435 was used for this service. The car is shown at Watts Carhouse, and will proceed to Torrance as the afternoon shop train. The man in the background is the shop foreman who is approaching to evict the photographer and a friend from the property. Somehow he was evaded and the two fans boarded the car and were able to ride the shop train. *(Ken Douglas)*

In the rebuilding program of 1946-48, ten Blimps were not equipped with the brake valves that would allow them to operate MU with the ex-NWP cars and the other 400 and 496 combos. They could run only with themselves. They were usually assigned to rush hour runs as the Long Beach Express or in special service to Santa Anita Race Track. As a consequence, they were the least used of the Blimps. Car 450 and train is shown climbing the ramp heading into the 6th and Main Street Station in downtown Los Angeles on September 12, 1949. The car carries no destination sign, and is likely a deadhead move coming from Macy Street Yard. Note the motorman is looking back to make sure the trolley poles remain on the wire. *(Henry Stange)*

PE 452 is shown outbound on the Southern District four tracks with a Long Beach line train at Florence Ave. on May 3, 1950. The white building in the far distance is the Los Angeles City Hall, for many years the tallest building in the city. This right of way is now used for the MTA Blue Line, and Florence Ave. is a station on the light rail line. *(Ken Douglas)*

The PE was able to purchase the motor trucks and electrical equipment from a number of USMC cars to motorize the ex-NWP Blimp trailers. The demotorized cars were then numbered 400-406 and used as operating trailers. After the war, they were assigned by the USMC to the Union Pacific and used behind steam locomotives in the Riverside area. They were later purchased by the PE in 1947 and used briefly and then sent to Torrance for cannibalization. USMC 406 became PE 4661 and was considered for rebuilding as a business car. The car is shown at Torrance on September 12, 1949 in a stripped condition. The plan came to naught, and the car continued to sit at the shop until it was scrapped in 1951. *(Henry Stange)*

The four former SP combos were modernized along with the rest of the Blimps in 1946-48 and numbered 496-499. PE 496 and 301 are shown at Macy Street Carhouse ready for a deadhead move downtown to Main Street Station on August 2, 1950. *(Jim Buckley)*

 Along with the coaches, the USMC also brought four SP combines to Southern California which were also taken over by the PE. PE 4700 and another unmodernized "Blimp" are shown southbound on the San Pedro line crossing the Manchester viaduct on the Southern District four tracks north of Watts in March, 1948. *(Ken Douglas)*

On December 29, 1948, PE combo 498 is shown with another 400 class car at Morgan Yard in Long Beach. The combos were acquired with the idea of using them to carry baggage on San Pedro and Santa Catalina boat trains. They were not heavily used however, and most were stripped for parts to use on the other cars. PE 498 was the last combo to remain servicable and lasted until the end of interurban service in 1961. The car is now preserved at the Orange Empire Railway Museum. *(Ken Douglas)*

The Pacific Electric was the very last operator of interurban Railway Post Office service. The final line, Los Angeles to San Bernardino was started on October 9, 1947. Weekdays RPO runs usually consisted of an RPO-Express and another Express car running MU, while Saturday trains used just the RPO-Express car. On April 9, 1949 PE 1406 with another box motor is shown operating outbound at City Terrace on the Los Angeles-San Bernardino train. *(Ken Douglas)*

PE 1406 is shown northbound on the Southern District four tracks at Washington Blvd. on September 22, 1951. At the time of this photo, mail service had ended, the RPO gear in the mail "apartment" and the special lettering had been removed and the car was operating as a straight box motor. *(Ken Douglas)*

The PE operated three trolley RPO-Express cars in the late 1940's. This view shows one of these at Macy St. Carhouse on September 19, 1948. Although the other two RPOs used during the period had been built as RPO cars, the 1407 had been rebuilt from a Portland passenger car when the 1404 was badly damaged by fire in a grade crossing accident in 1937. *(Ken Douglas)*

PE 1407 is shown at Baldwin Park in August, 1949 while running outbound to San Bernardino. The 1949 GMC pickup has delivered eastbound mail to the interurban, and will haul the inbound mail to the Baldwin Park post office. *(Emery Gulash)*

On the last day of Los Angeles-San Bernardino RPO service, May 5, 1950 a Saturday, the 1407 made the last run. The car is shown inbound from San Bernardino over the viaduct crossing the Santa Fe at Bench with the last run of a trolley RPO in the United States. *(Ken Douglas)*

PE 1422 is shown at Macy Street yard in July, 1949. This car is a relic of the 530-549 group of suburban cars called "Medium Fives". Although numbered in the box motor series, the car was used as a shop switcher at Macy St. Its mate, the 1423 was a paint car at Torrance Shops. *(Emery Gulash)*

In 1905-6 and 1910 the old PE built in its Los Angeles shops a group of wooden box motors. After the merger of 1911, the cars were numbered 1430-1444. The cars were capable of being used as locomotives, but in later years (because of full crew laws) were restricted to pulling another box motor or a steam road freight car as trailers. On Feb. 5, 1949, PE 1440 is shown running outbound on the Southern District four tracks. *(Emery Gulash)*

On May 20, 1949, PE 1441 is shown stored on the interchange tracks at the Southern Pacific station in Glendale. The SP mainline (running to Northern California) can be seen to the right. *(Emery Gulash)*

Pullman built in 1913 five steel box motors for the SP electric lines in Oregon. In 1927 and 1929 the cars were transferred to the PE and numbered 1445-1449. Car 1446 is shown on the Main Street Station surface tracks in September, 1952. By this time, the yard was used mostly for bus storage and on November 15, 1952 all box motor service on the Southern and Western Districts would end. *(William C. Janssen)*

PE 1447 is shown inbound on the San Bernardino line east of Valley Junction in March, 1948. Note the patch of fresh red paint around the MU receptacle just above the headlight. This indicates the relatively recent restoration of MU capability on this box motor for use on the San Bernardino RPO run which had been awarded to PE during this period. On the Monday to Friday RPO runs to San Berdoo, the RPO ran in MU with a box motor. *(Ken Douglas)*

Box motor 1448 is southbound on the San Pedro mainline at East Wilmington Junction with PE 1012 stopped by a signal coming off the Long Beach-San Pedro line on December 29, 1948. The box motor is carrying a white flag indicating it is an extra. Most PE box motor runs were operated as extra trains. *(Ken Douglas)*

After visiting San Pedro, Box motor 1448 is shown inbound at Wilmington Road Junction. At this point, the freight-only San Pedro via Gardena line leaves the West Basin line going north. To the left of the car, the West Basin line extends north and east of the junction with the direct line to San Pedro which ran over the Bascule Bridge over the connecting waterway into the West Basin of Los Angeles Harbor. *(Ken Douglas)*

Cars 1450-1456 were built by PE from 1915 to 1918. While resembling the earlier 1430 class, these cars had steel underframes, more powerful motors and were capable of operating on 1200-volts that was used on the San Bernardino line. The cars were provided with MU controls, but never operated in that mode as MU receptacles and jumpers were never installed. The cars often pulled other box motors and standard steam railroad boxcars. PE 1455 and another box motor are shown on April 9, 1949 north of Watts. Both trolley poles are on the wire to actuate grade crossing signals. *(Ken Douglas)*

PE 1452 is shown at the mail dock on the surface tracks under the 6th & Main elevated tracks on May 8, 1949. In previous years, the track on which 1452 is standing connected with PE tracks on 6th St. and was used by cars to reach points on the Western District. *(Ken Douglas)*

A need for more box motors caused the PE to convert two SP Oregon passenger cars into box motors 1457-1458. As with 1445-1449 the cars were equipped with MU in 1947 so that they could work with the RPO cars on the San Bernardino line. Car 1457 is shown stored at the Macy Street Carhouse on September 10, 1949. *(Henry Stange)*

On April 14, 1951, PE 1457 and 1446 are standing just west of the former Venice Short line crossing on the Santa Monica Air Line at Culver Junction. *(Ken Douglas)*

In 1941 the PE converted six more former SP Oregon passenger cars into box motors and numbered them 1459-1464. The rebuilding was not as thorough as previous conversions, all doors were retained, upper colored window sash was kept and the side windows were plated over by individual steel sheets. The cars were capable of operating only on 600-volts. Car 1459 is seen stored at 8th Street Yard on September 11, 1949 in the company of a 1450 type.
(Henry Stange)

The 1459 is seen again at the Monrovia Freight Station on November 21, 1950. The upper colored window sash left over from the days when the car carried passengers can be easily seen. At night, when the interior lights were on the light shining through these windows (that hadn't been painted over) was quite striking.
(Emery Gulash)

At the Los Angeles Union Passenger Terminal, the PE maintained a small yard off Aliso Street exclusively for box motors to load and unload baggage, express and less than carload freight from mainline Santa Fe, Southern Pacific and Union Pacific passenger trains. Car 1460 is seen in this yard with the terminal clock tower in the background on August 3, 1950.
(Jim Buckley)

PE 1463 is shown at Peach Street siding on the Santa Ana line on March 12, 1949. The photographer had the pleasure of an illegal ride on this box motor on the day the photo was taken. This car is another conversion of a Portland passenger car that was completed in 1941. *(Ken Douglas)*

The last PE box motor run on the Northern District was operated by PE 1463 when the car ran to Glendora on September 19, 1951. Box motor service to Pasadena and Alhambra had been abandoned on March 30, 1951. The car is shown at Glendora just before starting the last run inbound to Los Angeles. *(Ken Douglas)*

The largest box motors to operate on the PE were two cars acquired in 1942 from the SP Bay Area lines. Built by Pullman in 1913, the 1465 and 1466 were similar in many respects to the ex-SP coaches and combos that were also brought to Southern California (but under different circumstances). Car 1465 is shown running outbound to the south in Watts in September, 1952. Box motor service on the Southern and Western Districts will be abandoned on November 14, 1952. *(William C. Janssen)*

PE 1466 is running outbound on the Whittier line crossing Pacific Blvd. in Huntington Park on March 12, 1949. This shot is a favorite of the photographer since this is his hometown. He spent many a classroom hour in high school being alert to movements on this line, which was visible from school. This is the only time when the photographer saw one of the "Blimp Box Motors" on this line. *(Ken Douglas)*

The 1495-1499 group of box motors were converted from speedy 800-class passenger cars in 1940. Because of the press of WWII passenger requirements, they were reconverted to passenger cars with their original numbers for use on the Torrance Shop train. In 1945, the five cars were reconverted to box motors with the 1495-1499 numbers. Through all these conversions, the cars retained their MU capacity, the only PE wood box motors to be so equipped. Car 1495 is outbound between Flint and Pioneer Junction on December 29, 1948. This piece of track was the third leg of a wye which connected the San Pedro main and the Long Beach-San Pedro line just north of Wilmington station. *(Ken Douglas)*

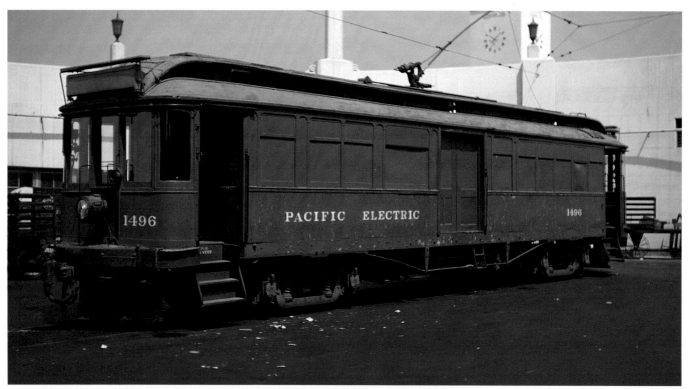

PE 1496 is being loaded at Los Angeles Union Passenger Terminal on August 3, 1950. Because of their speed, the converted "Eights" were often preferred for box motor runs over the 600-volt lines. *(Jim Buckley)*

The smallest and largest PE box motors are shown in this view of PE 1498 and 1466 taken on November 25, 1950 at Macy Street Yard. PE 1498 was rebuilt from an 800 that had been used on the Western District into the subway, and so was equipped with two trolley poles. After the need for this car had ended, PE donated the car to Travel Town in Los Angeles. *(Emery Gulash)*

4-52-4M

PACIFIC ELECTRIC RAILWAY COMPANY

S-5825

NOTICE OF REFUSED OR UNCLAIMED FREIGHT ON HAND DESTINATION

_____ 19___

Shipper_____   Station_____

Address_____   Agent's No._____

_____   Freight Bill No._____

DATE OF W. B.	W. B. NO.	CAR OR BOAT	B/L ISSUED BY	ORIGIN	DESTINATION

Shipper_____   Consignee_____

Commodity_____

The above described shipment arrived at destination_____, 19___ remains on hand undelivered account_____ with freight charges_____ advances_____ storage
(State reason for refusal or non-delivery)
accrued this date_____ and additional storage accruing daily at rate of_____

consignee notified of arrival on_____, 19___ by_____
(Show whether in writing, verbal, or postal)
Weight of shipment_____ present condition is_____

Actual value of same $_____ estimated $_____, shipper's

invoice number shown on tag attached to shipment is_____

As shippers are legally responsible for all unpaid freight charges on refused or unclaimed property will ask that you arrange for collection or payment of same, at same time furnish disposition of shipment as promptly as possible. When giving disposal orders, please accompany same with original bill of lading, or in lieu thereof execute a satisfactory indemnity bond duly signed. Prompt action is requested, otherwise shipment will be sold in accordance with section 4, of the Standard Uniform Bill of Lading.

cc: Consignee_____

_____ Destination Agent

Address_____   cc: Forwarding Agent_____

cc: Freight Claim Agent_____

TO AGENTS: Handle in accordance with instructions sending original of this notice to shipper, copy to consignee, copy to forwarding agent and copy to Freight Claim Agent.

In 1917, the PE acquired from the Southern Pacific a unique locomotive. The unit had been built in 1902 by the North Shore Ry., a predecessor of the Northwestern Pacific and named the *Electra*. In 1906 the locomotive was used for earthquake cleanup duties in San Francisco and then returned to the North Shore. At at unknown date, the locomotive was sold to the SP and later to the PE. The locomotive was used for a variety of tasks, but is best known for its work in helping to construct the PE subway in 1925, and later as a shop switcher at Torrance. After being stored for some years, the locomotive was retired in 1952 and donated to Travel Town in Los Angeles. The locomotive is shown on display there in 1964. *(Emery Gulash)*

Baldwin-Westinghouse built five Class B locomotives in 1920 for a Cuban sugar railway. Unable to make delivery, the locomotives were stored. In 1922 the PE purchased two and numbered them 1590-1591. The locomotives were smaller than the 1601-1618 type, but were perfectly suited for switching and short hauls running out of San Bernardino, and could run on 1200-volts. When the Eastern District was dieselized in 1943 by GE 44-tonners, the two units were brought to Los Angeles. No. 1590 is running outbound with a caboose hop on August 1, 1950 on the Southern District four tracks near Amoco. *(Jim Buckley)*

PE 1590 is seen on May 19, 1949 at the combined SP-PE freight station in Long Beach. Nos. 1590-1591 were retired in January, 1952 and were sold in 1953 to the F.C. General Urquiza in Argentina, where they are believed to still exist. *(Emery Gulash)*

Southern California's first steel electric locomotive was the 1600, built in 1905 by the old PE in the Los Angeles shops. Of 800HP, the unit was used primarily for switching in and around 8th Street Yard where it is shown on September 11, 1949 in the company of a Portland box motor. *(Henry Stange)*

PE 1600 is shown at 8th Street Yard switching on August 22, 1950. In 1923 the PE built a mate to the 1600, the 1599 which used the motors and controls from H. E. Huntington's private car, the *Alabama*. As can be seen, the motorman had an interesting "bucket seat" from which to watch the switchman. The locomotive was retired later in 1950, but copy 1599 was sold to Argentina where it was dismantled and used to construct a new locomotive. *(Ken Douglas)*

Outbound on the north to east leg of the wye at Slauson Junction in April, 1948, PE 1601 is moving east on the Whittier line on a short remaining section of double track between the junction and Holmes. PE locomotives were originally painted red, but after 1944 were painted black to follow SP diesel practice. Nos. 1601 was built by Baldwin-Westinghouse in 1912 and was of Model D. The locomotive would be retired in 1953 and scrapped. *(Ken Douglas)*

PE 1602 shows the SP "tiger stripe" paint scheme that was put on locomotives following SP practice. The 1912 Baldwin-Westinghouse is shown switching on the Santa Monica Air Line at Sentous on September 12, 1953. All of the 1601-1631 motors could operate on 600 or 1200-volts. *(Ray Ballash)*

By 1949, most of PE's locomotives had been painted black, but on May 8, 1949 the 1603 still carried red in the company of Portland Twelves and box motors at Macy Street Carhouse. *(Ken Douglas)*

In a once typical Southern California scene of tracks, trolley overhead and palm trees, PE 1610 is shown on September 25, 1953 on the Whittier line at Holmes Ave. In the right background, the standard PE "wig wag" crossing signal is warning traffic to stay clear of the electric locomotive. *(Ray Ballash)*

The PE often stored equipment at outlying locations when not in use. PE 1611, built by Baldwin-Westinghouse in 1913 is shown getting ready to start another work day in Santa Ana on December 1, 1951. The crew has raised the trolley pole and will shortly start inbound with a brand new Union Pacific boxcar and former Richmond Fredericksburg & Potomac caboose in tow. *(Ken Douglas)*

Later on, PE 1611 was used as a switcher at Butte Street Yard handling interchange traffic on Feb. 22, 1955. The fellow leaning against the handrail on the locomotive is the "trolley pup" whose primary function was to guide the trolley pole through the maze of overhead wires while switching in the yard. His job was more demanding when the pole was going backwards against the wire. *(Ray Ballash)*

In 1944, the PE started painting their locomotives black with white trim and lettering. 1612 is shown at Culver City in December 1948 with this scheme. The Baldwin-Westinghouse Class D locomotive had been built in 1916. *(Emery Gulash)*

In 1949, the PE started using black paint with orange striping following SP diesel painting practice. On September 11, 1949, the 1612 has obviously just been repainted into the new scheme when photographed stored at 8th Street Yard. *(Henry Stange)*

PE 1613 is shown drifting past the Watts Station on the Southern District four tracks in September, 1952. The locomotive is running outbound and will switch into the Watts Carhouse. *(William C. Janssen)*

Another Baldwin-Westinghouse locomotive that carried the red paint scheme very late was the 1614, shown stored at Culver City in December, 1948. *(Emery Gulash)*

Locomotives 1616 and 1617 were the last new Baldwin-Westinghouse locomotives to be acquired in 1920. At 65-tons they were the heaviest of all the B-W motors. No. 1616 is shown at Butte Street Yards in Los Angeles on November 26, 1953 in the company of a leased SP Baldwin VO-1000. PE rated the 1616 and 1617 as capable of pulling sixty cars. *(Ray Ballash)*

PE 1617 is shown inbound on the Venice Short Line near Vineyard Junction on August 4, 1950. The locomotive is about to deliver the flat car to a lumber yard near Vineyard. The location of the lumber yard gave it a competitive advantage since it was located near a residential area but could receive lumber by the carload. This would soon end, as on October 1, 1950 rail service would be abandoned on the VSL. *(Ken Douglas)*

When additional electric locomotives were needed, the PE found that it could construct locomotives cheaper than they could be obtained from commercial builders. Therefore, Nos. 1619-1631 were assembled by the PE at Torrance Shops in 1924-25. While they resembled the Baldwin-Westinghouse locomotives, they were equipped with General Electric equipment. No. 1620 is shown stored at the West Hollywood carhouse on April 24, 1954. *(Ray Ballash)*

Later in 1954, PE 1620 was used on the Southern District and is shown here at the Catalina Dock on November 11, 1954 switching in front of the steamship terminal. The caboose was acquired from the Richmond, Fredericksburg & Potomac. *(Ray Ballash)*

In 1945, MU equipment was installed on electric locomotives 1619-1631 to enable them to pull heavier trains on the San Bernardino line. 1621 and a sister are shown pulling a freight into San Bernardino from Colton on June 2, 1951. *(Sanford Goodrick)*

PE 1622 is shown resting in the shade of a tree (it gets warm in San Bernardino) on June 2, 1951 in the San Berdoo yard. On October 1st, the entire San Bernardino line into Los Angeles will be dieselized. *(Sanford Goodrick)*

After being moved to Los Angeles, the 1622 was used for Southern and Western District freight assignments. In an improbable view, the 1622 is shown in September, 1952 under clear skies, running over well kept ballast and a clean right of way into Watts over the four track right of way. Note the brand new PFE reefers behind the tank car. *(William C. Janssen)*

The Wingfoot Branch, which was operated in alternate years by PE and the Santa Fe, required the use of steam and diesel locomotives. Some track was electrified however, and could be used by PE electric equipment such as the 1625, shown here crossing Hooper Ave. on September 11, 1953. The "trolley pup" is doing his job of tending the trolley pole as the locomotive moves toward the camera with a string of box cars. *(Ray Ballash)*

PE 1626 is shown switching tower car 00161 and a PE single sheathed boxcar at Washington Street on the Southern District four tracks in February, 1956. The use of electric locomotives in this area would end on December 1st. *(Ray Ballash)*

While the electric locomotives of the 1619-1631 group could operate in multiple unit after 1945, that is not the case here as 1627 tows 1622 westbound on the San Bernardino line at San Dimas on October 30, 1949. PE required that each motor car or locomotive obtain power from its own pole, and did not use electrical jumpers or bus lines on freight equipment. *(Ken Douglas)*

PE 1627 and 1619 are shown running in multiple unit in September, 1952 on the Southern District four tracks with a rock train. The train is passing through Watts running southbound. *(William C. Janssen)*

Soon after a paint job, PE 1628 is shown switching a wood sheathed Fruit Growers Express reefer at Eighth Street Yard in Los Angeles in February, 1956. Electric freight operations here would be dieselized in December and the locomotive sold for scrap the following year. *(Ray Ballash)*

PE 1629 is shown stored at the West Hollywood carhouse on July 14, 1954. The locomotive was used at night to serve the freight spurs along Santa Monica Blvd. This service was to be the last electric freight operation on the PE, not being dieselized until January 8, 1958. While this particular locomotive was scrapped, the 1624 has been preserved at the Orange Empire Railway Museum. *(Emery Gulash)*

One of the more unlikely PE locomotives was the 1646. Built by Plymouth in 1932 as a Model HLB, type 2 for an interurban line in Ohio, the locomotive was leased to the PE in 1953 (and purchased in March, 1954) from parent SP, which had used it in Texas. The locomotive was too light for most assignments and was little used by the time it was photographed at the Watts Carhouse on July 20, 1957. This was not the smallest PE internal combustion locomotive, PE 1503, a shop switcher at Torrance was smaller. *(Edward S. Miller)*

At San Fernando, the PE operated an short freight line that was isolated from other PE trackage. To serve this "island", which connected with the SP, the railway operated a number of internal combustion locomotives. On November 11, 1953 PE was using the 1647, a Plymouth Model WLG six wheel locomotive. At this time, the PE was the fourth owner of the unit, which had been reengined with a diesel replacing its original gasoline engine. *(Ken Douglas)*

PE 1648 models the post 1944 black and white paint scheme when photographed on April 1, 1950 on the San Fernando "island". This unit was former Northwestern Pacific 903, a 72-foot long Brill gas-electric passenger- baggage combo. Brought down to the PE with the 904 in 1943, the units were too long to use as switchers, so were cut down at the Torrance Shops to make them more suitable. In this configuration they worked well enough to handle the two orphan lines at Orange and San Fernando. The expense and difficulty in maintaining the odd units was a deterrent for the PE to keep from purchasing three similar cars from the SP. *(Ken Douglas)*

In 1943 and 1944 the PE bought five General Electric 44-tonners. One was used around the docks at Long Beach, while the other dieselized the Eastern District. The other three were used on the Northern District. Before entering service, the units were equipped with trolley poles so that they could operate signals and crossing lights. No. 1653 is shown towing a leased SP diesel and caboose on the San Bernardino line on September 11, 1949. *(Henry Stange)*

The GE 44-tonners were found to be too light for many of the requirements of the PE. Owner SP would not allow the PE to purchase larger diesels, instead leasing their own units to the railway (while many of the 44-tonners were leased to the SP). In June, 1952, PE 1654 has replaced the 1647 and 1648 on the San Fernando "island". Note that the unit is still equipped with a trolley pole. *(Ray Ballash)*

The Wingfoot branch was opened in 1922, and was operated in alternate years by the PE (even numbered years) and Santa Fe (odd numbered years). To operate this line, the PE was required to use steam locomotives and purchased a small fleet to run over this line as well as non-electrified spurs on the Southern District. The PE also leased SP steam engines to use on this line, usually 0-6-0 switchers. In 1953, when PE operated the line steam was still used. The very last day of steam operation was on December 31, 1953 when leased SP 1239 was used to switch the line. This was the last use of steam on the PE, and the next day the Santa Fe took over operation of the line. *(Ray Ballash)*

PE 1022, a Baldwin Model VO-660 was leased from parent SP but lettered for PE when photographed on May 1, 1949 in Huntington Park on the Whittier line. Both 1021 and 1022 saw long time service on the PE after they were built in 1941. Both were eventually returned to the SP and sold for scrap in 1963. *(Ken Douglas)*

Another example of a leased Southern Pacific diesel lettered for the PE is PE 1320, shown on February 1, 1951 trundling over the Basset branch about to cross the severed San Bernardino line at Vineland near Baldwin Park. This track belonged to the SP prior to November 1946 when it was sold to the PE and electrified. PE 1320 is a Baldwin Model VO-1000 built in 1941. *(Ken Douglas)*

As late as 1956, when electric freight service ended on the Southern District, leased SP diesels used trolley poles to actuate signals. No. 1320, now lettered for the SP, is shown in June, 1956 running south on the four tracks with the trolley pole up. The 1320 would remain in ervice until September, 1964 when it was sold to General Electric as a trade in. *(Ray Ballash)*

PE 1326 is shown on December 31, 1949 running inbound on the Northern District four tracks near Topaz Street. The Baldwin VO-1000 was built in 1941 for the SP and was eventually returned to them. The locomotive was retired in 1962 and sold for scrap. *(Ken Douglas)*

The Pacific Electric in recent times numbered work cars with a zero or double zero prefix. Wrecker 002 is seen at Macy Street yard on September 10, 1949. This wrecker was rebuilt from box motor 1450 in 1920 when the need for a wrecker capable of 1200-volt operation on the San Bernardino line was recognized. *(Henry Stange)*

Wrecker 002 is shown inbound at Valley Junction on April 24, 1951 returning from a trouble call. After electric operations on the Northern District ended on October 1, 1951, the car was transferred to the Watts carhouse. The car served there until March 1953 when it was retired and later scrapped. *(Ken Douglas)*

PE 005 was another wrecker, rebuilt in 1948 from box motor 1438 which had been built in 1905. 005 was assigned primarily to West Hollywood carhouse, but also saw service on the Southern District. With the conversion of the Hollywood Blvd. line in 1954 the car was retired and given to the SP for disposal. *(Ken Douglas)*

This vehicle was one of two cars on the PE that could be used to put grease on the trolley wire. No. 00150 is shown at Macy Street yard on May 8, 1949. The greasing pole can be seen extending over the platform in the front. Sticks of grease were inserted in the housing attached to the trolley shoe and forced onto the wire with air pressure. Greasing the wire was required when slide trolleys replaced wheels. The other trolley system in Los Angeles, the yellow cars, used a carbon insert in the slide trolley, precluding the use of a wire greaser. *(Ken Douglas)*

PE 00150 was built by the Los Angeles Pacific in 1899. The car came to the PE in 1911 as tower car 1710, and was renumbered 00150 in 1931. The car was converted to a wire greaser in 1936 when PE adopted the use of steel shoes instead of trolley wheels for current pickup. The car is seen on August 4, 1950 outbound on the Venice Short Line on Venice Blvd. passing Loyola High School. Note that the car is using two trolley poles: the front pole is for power, and the rear trolley is for greasing the wire. This car made at least one trip a week over every line with passenger service. Greasing equipment was installed on other tower cars and this car was retired in 1958. 00150 is now preserved at the Orange Empire Ry. Museum. *(Ken Douglas)*

The trolley wire greaser is seen running on the Southern District four tracks at 60th St. on December 8, 1953. Only the PE, San Diego Electric and Lehigh Valley Transit in Pennsylvania are known to this writer as having trolley wire greasing cars, other electric railways preferring to use carbon insert trolley shoes. *(Ray Ballash)*

Tower cars were used by the PE for overhead wire maintenance. PE 00157 is shown inbound at San Marino on December 28, 1949. The tracks coming in from the left are the Sierra Madre line. The 00157 was considered the finest line car on the PE. Built in 1915 at the PE's Los Angeles shop, it was capable of being operated on the 1200-volt lines. The carbody is similar to the 1451 group of box motors and uses the massive Standard C-80P truck. *(Ken Douglas)*

PE 00157 was sent to the Southern District after electric operation on the Northern District ended in 1951. On the cool and rainy evening of November 5, 1953 the car is seen running on the four tracks at 60th Street. The car was in service until 1957 and is now preserved at the Orange Empire Ry. Museum. *(Ray Ballash)*

One of the more interesting tower cars was the 00160, shown here at Torrance Shops on September 12, 1949 after it was retired. The car was built as a streetcar for service in New York City. The Los Angeles Pacific purchased ten of these cars from the Third Ave. Ry. right after the turn of the century. Used as passenger cars for a very brief period on the LAP, all were converted to non-passenger uses. This car was converted to an express car by the LAP and was used as a box motor after the Great Merger. Converted to a tower car in 1924 the car was renumbered 1733, and to 00160 in 1931. There were a total of three of these tower cars with a similar history and all became line cars. PE historian Ira Swett called the tower platform a "Pagoda". *(Emery Gulash)*

PE 00161 was built by the PE in 1923 and was similar to the 00157 but could only operate on 600-volts and was stationed on the Southern District. The car is seen here on December 28, 1949 at the Washington Blvd. Engineering Yard. The car operated until the conversion of the Long Beach Line in 1961. This car has been preserved by The Red Car Museum in Seal Beach, California. *(Ken Douglas)*

The last tower car built was the 00162, built by the PE in 1929 to provide the company a second tower car capable of operating on 1200-volts. The car was stationed at San Bernardino and later brought to Macy Street where it is seen on September 19, 1948. After the abandonment of all electric service on the Northern District, the 00162 was used to take down the trolley wire. During the latter stages of this melancholy task, it was pulled around by a diesel-electric. *(Ken Douglas)*

In 1939, the PE converted box motor 1414 into tower car 00164. The car was stationed at Washington St. on the Southern District until 1950 and then assigned to the West Hollywood carhouse as it was then the only tower car with a profile compact enough to operate in the PE subway. The car is seen here at West Hollywood on January 15, 1950. *(Ken Douglas)*

With the abandonment of the Hollywood Blvd. line, the 00164 was transferred to Toluca Yard at the mouth of the subway so that it could be used to maintain the wires on the remaining Western District operation, the Glendale-Burbank line. The car was also used as a wrecker and locomotive to switch the tool car (an old box car) at this location. The car is seen at Toluca on June 16, 1955. In a few more days, on the 19th, the Glendale-Burbank line will be converted to bus and the car will be used to remove the overhead over the extensive private right of way of the line. *(Emery Gulash)*

The PE constructed eight portable substation cars for use when the demands for power exceeded fixed substation capacity. PE 00186 was built during World War Two by PE for the U.S. Maritime Commission, and sold later to the PE. The car is shown here on August 14, 1954 while stationed at Dominguez Junction. Most portable substations were painted green in later years. *(Ray Ballash)*

Portable substations 00187 and 00182 are shown stored at Washington Street Engineering Yard on July 30, 1953. When needed, the cars will be towed by a locomotive to their area of use, and will be blocked and leveled to enable the machinery to operate a maximum efficiency. In later years, these cars were semi-permanently stationed at various locations, and had structural additions made to them, such as walkways and platforms. *(Ray Ballash)*

PE 00190 was a small crane, stationed at West Hollywood carhouse where it was photographed on January 15, 1950. The car was built as a single truck tower car by the "old" PE in 1902. In 1911 the car became number 1700 and was converted to a crane in 1916. The car became 00190 in 1931 and was scrapped in 1950.
(Ken Douglas)

Yet another crane, although much larger was the 00191. This car was built by the Los Angeles Pacific as an electric shovel, and came to the PE in 1911 as No. 1820. The car was converted to a crane by the PE and numbered 00191 in 1931. The crane was used all over the 600-volt system and was self propelled. The car was named "The Cherry Picker" and was painted gray. The car was also PE's only powered car that was used on the mainline that didn't have pilots or foot-boards. The car is seen here dismantling the Sierra Madre line at California Ave. near Lamanda Park on Feb. 1, 1951.
(Ken Douglas)

The business end of the 00191 is seen on Feb. 1, 1951 while lifting rail onto a flat car from the Sierra Madre line at California Ave. Box motor 1451 is providing motive power for the flat cars.
(Ken Douglas)

The Pacific Electric also owned a steam crane, No. 00194 built by the Ohio Locomotive Crane Co. in 1922. The crane has been moved over the Santa Monica Air line to Ocean Park on December 27, 1950 and is performing construction work so that a new bus garage can be built at this location.
(Ken Douglas)

One of PE's smallest motor cars was the 00196, which was used as one of the Torrance Shop switchers. built by old PE in 1902, car became 1510 and 00196 in 1940. The car is seen here "chaining" a 1000-series car to pull it under overhead so the car can be moved into the Torrance Shops to be scrapped on September 12, 1949. *(Henry Stange)*

The 00196 is shown in a different view also taken at Torrance on September 12, 1949. One would think the bucket seat to improve operator vision would not be needed on a car with no windows, hoods or other impediments to vision. The car was scrapped in 1955. *(Henry Stange)*

Yet another tiny motor car was the 00197, the West Hollywood sand car. The car is believed to have been built in 1895 for the Los Angeles & Pasadena Electric Ry., a PE predecessor. Numbered 1516, PE used the car as a shop switcher until 1940 when it was made into a sand car. The car is shown at West Hollywood on April 14, 1954. The car was sent to Travel Town, but is now at the Los Angeles County Museum in Exposition Park. *(Ray Ballash)*

In 1948, the PE purchased a Brownhoist electric crane from the San Diego Transit System. The crane had been built in 1922 and was former SDTS and San Diego Electric Ry. No. 022. The car was assigned to Torrance Shops where it is seen on July 23, 1953. *(Ray Ballash)*

Also in 1948, the PE decided that it needed a rail grinder to reduce rail corrugations in heavy traffic areas, although the railway had not previously owned a rail grinder. Former interurban 1001 was converted to rail grinder 00199. The car was successful and was stationed at West Hollywood where it was photographed on April 1, 1950. The car was sold to Mr. Walter Abbenseth and has been restored to PE 1001 at the Orange Empire Ry. Museum. *(Ken Douglas)*

PE 0900 is a Differential Dump Car built in 1928. One of two motor cars (along with 0901) the cars were used to pull seven Differential dump trailers built at the same time. The cars were used to carry ballast and waste for track jobs. The car is shown at the Torrance Shop on September 12, 1949. *(Henry Stange)*

The PE also operated off road M/W equipment including this ancient gasoline roller seen at Macy Street Yard in 1960. *(Ray Ballash)*

After World War Two, the PE was forced to purchase conventional cabooses to replace older equipment. One group was acquired from the Lehigh Valley. No. 1971 is an example of a former LV car. The view was taken at the Orange Empire Ry. Museum where the car is preserved. *(Emery Gulash)*

The Pacific Electric operated a large fleet of standard steam railroad freight cars, most of them based on SP designs. Many were transferred to the SP for use elsewhere, but a number remained on the PE. In later years, all were assigned to the M/W series. No. 00119, a former SP Class B-50-14 car that came from the 10000-100599 series is seen at Perris. *(Emery Gulash)*

In the 1940s, the White Model 798 was the most numerous motor coach on the PE. Acquired from 1941 through 1948, the gasoline powered coach was primarily purchased to replace older motor coach equipment and for increased traffic caused by World War Two. No. 2075 was built in 1941 with 45-seats. When new, PE Whites were painted red with silver roofs and orange "wings", but after 1950 many were repainted into the "teardrop" scheme first developed for the GMC TDH-5103 coaches.
(Eli Bail Collection)

The PE was not the only electric railway to run in Los Angeles. The Los Angeles Transit Lines (Los Angeles Railway before 1945) ran an extensive rail system in Los Angeles that gave the PE stiff competition on many of the local routes. The LATL streetcars were 3'6" gauge (the PE was standard), so the vehicles of one company could not run on the other. When the routes of the two companies shared streets and right of way, it was necessary for a third rail to be installed. Among the oldest LATL streetcars still operating were the BF and BG types that ran on the "N" line, converted to bus in 1950. One of these cars is shown at Main and First in Los Angeles on September 10, 1949. The curved tracks in the foreground were used by the PE Watts-Sierra Vista Line. (*Henry Stange*)

By the early 1950's the most prevalent type of car on the LATL was the H-4 type, built in the 1920s. The very first car of this series, No. 1201 is running on 7th Street on the "S" line on September 10, 1949. Curving in front of the photographer are PE tracks going into the Main Street Station surface tracks, used by this time for car storage and box motors. *(Henry Stange)*

On the North side of the Los Angeles Union Passenger Terminal, LATL had a loop to load and unload passengers. Car 1444 and another are shown at this facility on July 14, 1954. *(W. C. Janssen)*

LATL 1501 looks like a Class H car, but is in fact a wooden copy built by the Los Angeles Railway in 1923-1924. After conversion to one-man/two-man service in the 1930's, the car type was known as class K-4. The car is shown at the northern terminal of the "7" line on Spring Street at Sunset on September 10, 1949. *(Henry Stange)*

The LATL also operated PCC cars, 165 of them. LATL 3107 running on the "J" line is shown on 7th Street on September 10, 1949. The Blimps following are coming out of Seventh Street surface yard and will go around the block to enter Main Street Station. *(Henry Stange)*

The most modern LATL cars were 40 PCCs that were built in 1948. Car 3154 is shown running running outbound on the P line on First Street passing a similar car. As with Metro Coach, Los Angeles Transit Lines was taken over by the Los Angeles Metropolitan Transit Authority on March 3, 1958. The narrow gauge PCCs ran until 1963, when streetcar and trolley coach service was replaced by diesel bus. *(W. C. Janssen)*

Not exactly a competitor to the PE or LATL, was the Angels Flight Ry. This cable line opened in 1901 and ran up Bunker Hill from Hill and 3rd St. using two cars named *Olivet* and *Sinai*. The line was eventually closed due to urban renewal, but has been restored in a slightly different location and is in operation today. PE and LATL cars ran by the incline on Hill Street. The entire length of the incline can be seen in this view taken on September 10, 1949. *(Henry Stange)*

After the abandonment of the LA-Redondo Beach via Playa Del Ray line in 1940, a short section was left in place between Culver Junction and Alla for freight service. This view shows the actual end of track and overhead on this remnant, facing west toward the haze and the Pacific Ocean on July 26, 1953. *(Ray Ballash)*